A Scottish Childhood

— VOLUME II —

MORE FAMOUS SCOTS REMINISCE

Compiled by

Nancy E. M. Bailey

HarperCollins*Publishers*

HarperCollins Publishers
P.O. Box, Glasgow G4 0NB

First published 1998

© The Scottish Council of Save the Children, 1998

ISBN 0 00 472176 4

10 9 8 7 6 5 4 3 2 1 0

Printed and bound in Great Britain by
Caledonian International Book Manufacturing Ltd, Glasgow

Contents

CONTENTS

BUCKINGHAM PALACE

A Scottish Childhood Volume II offers more fascinating insights into days gone by, and many of the memories cover the time around the Second World War.

Most of the children were protected by loving parents and the extended family, and played with a freedom that most modern children can only dream about. The boys all seemed to play footie, 'keepie uppie', made boats, and went to scout camp. The girls' stories are slightly different: longing to wear a kilt like a brother, but relegated to the dreaded party dress, and learning by stealth that women can write.

The generosity of the wide range of contributors in sharing their stories means that some of the world's most deprived children will enjoy their childhood a little more; every copy of the book sold will generate a donation for Save the Children.

Anne

Introduction

❦

The notion that childhood is special and precious is a modern one. We no longer see children solely as miniature adults who need teaching, correction and guidance to set them on their predetermined path through life. This transition is part of the story to be found in *A Scottish Childhood*.

The contributors to this volume come from all parts of Scotland and from all walks of life. Some grew up on estates with ponies and traps, some grew up in crowded Glasgow single ends and some on island farms. There are incomers here, too, who found themselves unexpectedly in a Scotland which appeared terribly foreign in speech and habit.

Many of the stories and situations will be broadly familiar to anyone who grew up in the 'First World' during this century. Indeed, much of their charm comes from this universality of experience. How, then, can it be called a *Scottish* childhood? It is unlikely that Scottishness can be defined by the number of games of 'keepie-uppie' played down closes, or the commitment to memory of the national football squad, although it seems that nearly every boy (and many girls) spent a great deal of time doing just that. Is it embodied in a fierce sense of justice or a desire to make something of oneself, even at the risk of being set apart? Is it simply to be found in centuries-deep layers of shared cultural experience and expectation? The answer, of course, is that it is all of these things, and undoubtedly many others besides.

What is described in *A Scottish Childhood* is almost a cliché: the close-knit communities, the strong extended family bonds, a child's unquestioning assumption of the rightness of his or her place in the scheme of things. Not that every story describes a childhood of happiness, ease and plenty. Appalling things happened to children, then as now. The struggles to find a voice where closeness has become claustrophobic, to find acceptance as a stranger, to understand the unwritten rules which unaccountably set one group against another — these are here, too. It is in their variety that these stories can all be called *A Scottish Childhood*.

Nancy E.M. Bailey
Killearn, 1998

Acknowledgments

❦

When James Carney from HarperCollins sat with me in my sunny garden in July 1997 and asked me if I would be interested in editing this book, I was both delighted and apprehensive. Delighted, obviously, that I would be doing something concrete to help Save the Children, but apprehensive too, because – as anyone who has ever heard me immediately realises – I did not have a Scottish childhood.

Luckily for me, all the contributors to this volume have been able to speak quite easily for themselves. It is their willingness to give their most precious commodity, their time, to *A Scottish Childhood Volume II* which makes this book so heartwarming.

It is also fair to say that this book would never have seen the light of day without the support of Beryl Fitzpatrick, Save the Children's Scottish Regional Manager and Belinda Lennie, the Scottish Council Secretary. It has been a pleasure to work closely with Belinda who remained unflappable in the face of the unexpected and who was always able to devise new ways to approach and convince prospective contributors that they did have a story to tell. My thanks go to them all.

Thanks are also due to the publishers who kindly granted permission for extracts from books on their lists to be featured. Specifically,

Canongate Books Ltd, 14 High St, Edinburgh for the extract from *Weir's World* by Tom Weir (1994)

Random House for the extract from *Good Vibrations* by Evelyn Glennie and Pamela Norris (1990)

Mainstream Publishing for the extracts from *High Balls and Happy Hours* by Gavin Hastings and Clem Thomas (1994) and *East End to West End* by John Cairney (1988)

Weidenfeld and Nicolson for the extracts from *The Straight Man – My Life in Comedy* by Nicholas Parsons (1994) and *One Foot on the Stage: the biography of Richard Wilson* by Richard Wilson and James Roose-Evans (1996)

Glasgow City Libraries and Archives for the extract from *Rescue His Business, The Clyde His Life* by George Parsonage

Tom Weir

❧

Rolls and Drum Rolls

At 12 years of age you could get a job as a milk-boy in our nearest Co-operative dairy, starting at 6 a.m.; pay, three shillings a week. I followed my brother Willie who warned me that as a new boy I would be put through the mill on my first morning. He was right. As I got to the darkened dairy before the milkmaids arrived I was grabbed, stuffed into a wicker basket designed to hold morning rolls, and promised I would certainly get a roll.

Clamped in darkness I was dragged at a steep angle up a stair, then another stair. 'Now you'll get your roll!' they shouted as they launched me from the landing, the hamper turning over and over, with me inside it, as it crashed to the first landing, then to the bottom, where, a bit dazed, I was dragged out. Now I had to run the gauntlet between two rows of boys, each having a skelp at me with the hard skip of his skull-cap. In due course I had the pleasure of being a hamper-tosser to a succession of new boys as the old ones were compulsorily retired when they reached school-leaving age at 14.

As a lad I found the noise and stir of Springburn exciting. Each morning an army of locomotive workmen, 10,000 strong, answered the shriek of hooters, the noise of their heavy boots clattering on the pavements, all in a hurry and in a uniform of dungarees. Noisy tramcars, bells clanging, would be chuntering up and down Springburn Road where shops of every kind faced each other, many of them bearing the logo of Cowlairs Co-operative Society.

There was also the 148th Boys' Brigade Company available for 12-year-olds. It was a great day for me when I got in and was given a rope-tensioned side drum just a bit long for a wee fellow like me. It tended to bounce up and down on my knee when I was beating it out behind the pipers and my secret fear was that the drum would bounce off its attachment hook one day. That dread was realised on a very important occasion when Springburn Hill was lined with admiring watchers. Pipes skirling, we were descending to link with other companies to celebrate the birth of the Boys' Brigade movement. Then it happened! The drum was off and bouncing on the road with the smallest drummer on parade running after it. I was mortified, especially as the laughter was louder in my ears than the bagpipes.

From Weir's World - An Autobiography of Sorts

Tom Weir MBE (born 1914) is a world traveller, climber, photographer, writer and naturalist.

Francis David Charteris

❦

Travel Mishaps

I am not a great writer, and I have now, at the age of 85, a poorish memory. I did not have a particularly dramatic childhood, but I do actually remember one incident which could possibly have ended in real disaster, caused by a fall from a pony cart.

At Gosford at the time this incident occurred, which must have been during the First World War, perhaps 1917, we had a charming but skittish pony called Kitty. I used to ride on her. In fact, she used to draw my great-grandfather around in his wheelchair. He had been born in 1818, had lovely white side whiskers, and died in 1914 aged 95. His 96th birthday, had he had it, was 4th August, the day the war started, and I have always been glad he was spared that. We have a photograph of the Four Generations: him; my grandfather, Hugo; my father, Hugo (always called Ego); and myself aged 7 or 8 months.

Kitty used to draw the pony cart. There was, and still is, a house called Harestanes on the coast, at the west end of Kilspindie Golf Course. The official approach to it was via the Bulwark Road, which ran along the shore from a point near the main entrance to Gosford, and led to the Golf Course and Harestanes, and later to

Green Craig, which my cousin, Maurice Yorke, started building in 1923.

The road was supported on great rocks piled up from the sea, and it faced about due west so enjoyed all the storms rushing down the Firth of Forth. It is just about destroyed now and the bushes from the adjoining Harestanes Wood have encroached on the remains. A few years later they enlarged and improved the sand track through the wood. That road, now tarmacadamed, is now the proper route to Harestanes and Green Craig. On the day I speak of we were going, as often, to have tea at Harestanes. There was, I think, my brother Martin and I, my grandmother's secretary, Winifred Wilkinson, and Nettie Parratt, who was driving. Probably the pony was a bit mettlesome, but anyhow for some reason the left wheel of the carriage went over the edge of the bulwark, and we were stuck at a frightening angle. All was well, however: somebody hove the wheel up again and righted the pony cart, and we proceeded on our way on the level. Of course, I was not frightened!

Another story concerns our return from South Uist in September 1922. I went fairly often to Grogarry Lodge there, which was rented for many years by the Bensons, my step-father's family. Connection with the mainland was by the MacBrayne steamer *Plover*, a small, inadequate vessel with a permanent list to port. She was based at the Kyle of Lochalsh, and went round Skye three times a week, once clockwise and twice widdershins, each turn taking the inside of two days. The best way of getting to South Uist from the south was to catch her at Mallaig at about 1 p.m. on Monday, and the best way of getting back was to board her at Lochboisdale at about midnight Friday/Saturday, go direct to Mallaig and catch the last train of the week at about 1 o'clock.

This particular time there was a severe 'Equinoctial' gale, and the *Plover* was very late. I don't know where she spent her lost time, but it was well after daylight when she got to Lochboisdale, and we feared we would miss the train. In spite of telegrams to the Station Master, prayers to Heaven, and a strong westerly gale, so we did! There was a war on between MacBrayne and the London and North-Eastern Railway Company, and the latter had not the helpful attitude we all hoped for. The train left Mallaig most punctually, and as we entered the harbour all we saw was the plume of white smoke disappearing along the coast line.

Distress and fury all round, of course. No train until Monday morning, no motor cars to speak of, and the very primitive road was probably flooded. I believe this was the time when somebody called the Station Master a blood-orange! We were stuck for two nights in the Hotel, and many of our fellow passengers could not afford even that. Sunday was spent watching the gannets diving into the raging waters of the sea. I have never since ceased to glory in the spectacle, and to admire the way they do it.

Although this drama caused great inconvenience to numerous holiday makers from Glasgow and elsewhere, it helped lead to improvements to communications on the West Coast.

Francis David Charteris (born 1912), Earl of Wemyss and March KT, served for seven years in the Colonial Service in Basutoland (now Lesotho) and saw war service in the Middle East. He is Lord Clerk Register of Scotland, Keeper of the Signet, and Custodian of the Stone of Destiny.

Marion Campbell

First Time on Any Stage

I was not an only child, I was the survivor of three, not much indulged but surrounded by love. It seems odd, then, that the early memories are of outraged hullabaloo.

There was a vast pink-tinged horse-chestnut candle swaying above the pram; there was a figure vanishing beyond the hedge; appallingly, there was the World's Biggest Bumble Bee in that blossom and about to move elsewhere... End of that bright hope of settling Baby for her nap.

I had dear friends; Catherine (of the pram) and Sandy, reluctant convert from Coachman to Chauffeur, always clicking encouragement to his engine before allowing it a lower gear. Sandy made miraculous gondolas from folded iris leaves, or played cockabandie (a kind of skittles) with fir cones. Less happily, when the motor-car balked on a brae and all adult passengers were decanted to push, I was left in the driving seat to 'hang on to the wheel'. I could scarcely reach it, and it kicked with Model-T vigour. When we sailed triumphantly over the crest, I never trusted the pushers to get back aboard before we shot down the next slope: I was convinced that we would be blown over exposed headlands, or (with rather more reason) blown sky-high by one of the frequent backfires. It was not a luxury car — a wooden waggonette body on a standard Ford chassis, two lengthwise seats with slippery leatherette cushions, and a low centre-back door above an iron step which bit one's legs as one was lifted aboard. The sides were of canvas, buttoned around iron stanchions, with little talc peepholes too high for me. And one terrible day that low door nearly lost me another friend.

I had selected Mrs Noah as my companion for whatever expedition was underway. She was very like a clothespeg, with a round head to fit the mouth and an overall colour scheme of a pleasing indigo (doubtless lead-based, like all the Ark, but I was not the first child to survive that). As we banged along, Mrs Noah lay snugly in the pocket of my knitted coat, but some busybody must have vetoed hands in pockets, for out she came and over the little door.

The uproar stopped Sandy the moment we reached a level, but nobody knew what was wrong and I was incoherent. At last they gathered that something had fallen out, and we all climbed down to search for a 'mystery object'. By good luck, the Labrador was of the party, dear Susan, who realised the puppy had dropped its treasure and began a careful snuffle down the roadside. It was she, of course, who restored Mrs Noah to me; she was already my particular friend (had she not taught me to shake hands?) and thereafter she was special indeed.

But Catherine left to get married, or so they said; I told her not to, but though she wept, she didn't listen. If she had stayed, the next disaster might have been averted.

Mother was recovering from a serious illness, the annual Ploughing Match was coming, people didn't want Mother to catch cold giving out the prizes. Of course, Mrs A. might have stood in, or Aunt C. could have come to stay, or at a pinch Lady G. — but any of them would at least have to be asked to luncheon (not 'lunch', dear), and Mother would feel obliged to escort them to the field, which would defeat the whole object. Somebody — and I strongly suspect Father — proposed that I could perfectly well hand over a few prizes; heaven knew I'd have to do it often so I might as well start early. He'd look after me, Sandy would look after me, I knew most of the people already. Surely to goodness I could learn a few simple words to say?

I was looking forward to the Ploughing Match, and had already exerted influence, being sent into the committee meeting to hand over Mother's regular special prizes: a handsome black tie for 'Oldest Ploughman' and an equally plump and glossy navy blue tie for 'Oldest Unmarried Ploughman'. It was uncivil of the Committee to fall about when I stomped in and told them, 'that's for Colin and that's for Dunkie' which they must have known, but committees are unruly creatures and should not be taken seriously.

Meanwhile, those 'few words' were being taken all too seriously. I was at that stage bilingual, with a preference for Gaelic and a good accent (thanks to Father and Catherine), however limited by vocabulary. Mother had no Gaelic, hard as she tried to learn, so it fell to Cook to coach me. Every morning when she and Mother had toured the larders and drawn up the menu, I was sat on the broad windowsill and put through my paces, with a ginger biscuit in the offing. Mother could not assess content or style; Father did not attend rehearsals.

Came the great day, a raw February day, hard on horse and man, a bitter wind bringing heavy showers to an exposed field, a long contest on ground growing heavier by the hour. I waited impatiently indoors until Sandy fetched me late in the afternoon, so I saw nothing of the great and beautiful horses. Wrapped and buttoned to the eyeballs, I was hurried to the coach house whence the car had been displaced and where a stable lantern dimly lit the prize table. When the whole company pressed into shelter the prize giver was invisible — and retains an image of sleety stair-rods driving beyond a huddled mass of faceless forms.

Not one to be easy beat, as he said himself, Sandy turned over a laundry basket and stood me on it, but it wasn't high enough so he added his car-washing pail and set me on top of all. The basket rocked on its two handles, the bucket wobbled and was barely wide enough for two damp feet in square-toed shoes (children's wellies were scarcely known, and anyway were not approved: they 'drew your feet'). Sandy held me on the left, Father on the right, a hush fell, and I launched into my opening phrase: Tha mi glé-thoilichte a'bhith faicinn sibh a'rithis ('I am very pleased to see you again'), words with which many a laird's or minister's wife had welcomed people to many a Sale of Work in Cook's experience. Rolling from the lips of a stout woollen bundle, the effect was totally absurd. There was no more Speech, I have no idea what further gems had been planned; after a stunned moment, I was virtually blown off my bucket by a gale of laughter.

I was black affrontit, and so was Sandy, who removed me first to Mrs Sandy's fireside and thence homeward when consoled. I knew not nor cared how they all got their prizes, the Cup and the Best-Turned-Out-Pair, the Best Finish and the others, including, of course, the Oldest and Oldest Unmarried Ploughmen. I know Father was overcome with remorse, and feared I would never face another audience. I have faced a few since then; there may be something to be said for getting the worst over first.

Marion Campbell of Kilberry (born 1919) is a professional writer and amateur archaeologist.

Jamie Stuart

Prize Baby

The midwife smiled. My wee naked body was safely delivered into her eager hands. There had been no stress — but yes, some blood, sweat and tears. Let me tell you about the tears.

The date was 10th September 1920. I had two brothers — John and Peter — six years and three years old respectively. My mother had always been desperate for a girl and had hoped fervently that the good Lord would answer her prayer. Surely number three would meet her heart's desire?

'Well now, Mrs Stuart,' said the midwife, 'You can have a shot now. There you are, lassie — a lovely big boy!' Hear this dear readers: my mother burst into tears and wept uncontrollably for several minutes.

Doctor McNab came forward. 'Dear me! Dear me! What's all this carry-on about, Mrs Stuart? What's vexing you?' 'I'm fine, Doctor,' my mother replied, blowing her nose furiously, 'but, ye see, I wanted a wee girl this time.' And the wailing increased in volume. 'Mrs Stuart,' said the Doc, 'you should be ashamed of yourself. We've had no trouble at all, and you have at your bosom a lovely healthy boy. He looks great. I'll tell you this — you are the mother of a Prize Baby!'

My mother, bless her heart, in a kind of way lived to regret telling me the story of my entry into the world. Whenever she had cause to reprimand me for any reason, I would remind her that I was her Prize Baby! This usually prompted a smart scud in the rear end, and I would get the message. (By the way, the last addition to the family was also a boy!)

The doctor's forecast was accurate. In later years, I did indeed win prizes: as an athlete in track and cross-country running. In 1948, at Hampden Park in the Scottish Amateur Athletic Championships I won the two-mile steeplechase title.

However, my earliest recollection of attempting success (and of winning a prize!) in an exam was a disaster. In 1928, our family lived in a pleasant wee village called Stepps just ten miles from Glasgow. Each Sunday that God sent I had to satisfy my Mum and Dad that the back of my neck and ears were scrubbed, my ginger hair was slicked down, and my boots were well polished. The bells were ringing: Mr and Mrs Stuart and their four lads marched proudly to the Kirk.

For some reason or another I was not a member of the Sunday School. I don't know why this was the case. I've no doubt my parents were busy enough coping with life in hard times. Our only connection with the Church was the Sunday morning service and I didn't think to question my parents about Sunday School. Church attendance was a great joy for me. I loved the atmosphere and the dignity of all concerned. The sermons were long and I certainly didn't understand them, but my attention was alerted one year when the Sunday School Bible Exam prizes were presented. I decided that I, too, would be fair proud to step up to the front of the Kirk and receive a prize.

The following spring, a pulpit intimation was read out stating that the Bible exams would be held in the Church Hall on the first Saturday of the next month at 3 p.m. I was 8-years-old. I desperately wanted to win a prize and to shake hands with the Minister's wife.

The important day arrived and I reported at the Church Hall. The teachers seemed surprised to see me. Who could blame them? I wasn't a member of the Sunday School and had not received instructions or preparation to equip me for the test. Even so, I was directed to a desk, upon which lay several sheets of white paper, a pen and a pot of ink. At one minute to three, the question paper was handed out and sharp at three the bell was rung. My first action was dead easy. I wrote my name and age at the top of the first sheet. I read the first question and realised I couldn't answer it; likewise the second question, and the third, and so on to the end of the paper. I was totally out of my depth. I knew nothing. The other boys and girls were writing away furiously. I blew my nose for something to do. My face was red. I could feel it burning. My wee head was bursting. I was in agony. The tears splashed onto the virgin paper — well, not quite: it had my name and age.

A teacher noticed my torment and quietly asked if I was not well. I mimed to her that I had a headache, and without making eye contact with anyone I tip-toed my way to the exit door. Outside I breathed the fresh air of an escaped prisoner. My Mum and Dad knew nothing of my doings and I never informed a living soul about that sorry day.

Jamie Stuart (born 1920) is an actor and the author of
A *Glasgow Bible*.

George Wyllie

❦

Impossible Beginnings

A young man once told me about an idea that he and his friends had when they were still at school. They had come across an old door and they decided they'd like to convert it into a surfboard. One of them nicked his Dad's jig-saw and shaped the door into an oval. Then they collected loads of old polythene packaging and strapped it to the underside of the door for buoyancy. It took them two days to complete their work, and then he remembers standing back to admire the masterpiece... it was so funny... all they saw was a heap of junk that none of them would have been seen dead on down at the beach. They never did launch their stupid surfboard and the door ended up being dumped. Looking back, it was a great adventure — no sense of direction, just invention and intuition.

His story reminded me of my schooldays, when I was mad about flying. I wanted to build a glider — a flying wing with a sort of sledge-like undercarriage — the nearest I could get to making an aeroplane. I nicked a couple of long pieces of wood for the leading and trailing edges of the wing, which I covered with thick brown paper, like making a big kite. The take-off was a big adventure. Near where I lived there was a very steep slope and a sandy gully down the middle, which would keep me in the right downward direction. I reckoned that by travelling down the slope I would gather speed, then take off and fly. I pushed myself off and descended at high speed in a cloud of brown dust — but I never got off the ground and came to a bumpy stop at the bottom. I had no fear when I did this, and I can only recollect doing it once, yet I remember the quick precarious downward slide so well.

My glider was as laughable as my friend's surfboard, but both hopeless experiments seemed to be driven by unquestioned optimism, and a very doubtful sense of direction and intuition. I reckon now that we would both agree that possibilities which might be made to happen start with impossible beginnings. Possibilities can, and usually do, happen later — but great adventures can happen all the time.

George Wyllie (born 1921) made the 'Straw Locomotive' and the 'Paper Boat' sculptures, wrote and performed A *Day Down a Goldmine* and A *Voyage Round a Safety Pin* and founded Scul?ture and Synenergezetics, which embraces everything anywhere.

Ian Hamilton

Learning the Hard Way

The day I put my hand up Myfanwy's skirt was the day I stopped believing in grown-up wisdom. She was five and I was four, and the rattle I got on my ear sounds down through 65 years like Big Ben itself. All I wanted was information. We were in our first term at school. We sat together. I had been told that boys were different from girls and I wanted to find out where and why. I had also been told that girls were little ladies who had to be treated gently and didn't have the strength of boys. The belt on the ear belied that. Soon we became quite friendly. Girls, even five-year-old girls, respect bold four-year-old boys. I wonder where she is now? Nothing I did harmed her. But what about me? I've never taken a liberty since with a woman of any age unless she has asked me first — preferably in writing.

Of course telling you about Myfanway is not the only secret I'm going to let go. There were Peggie and Wilma and Celia and Winnie, with all of whom I was at one time desperately and blamelessly in love, blamelessly because of that clout I got as a four-year-old. Few write about the early loves of childhood. Perhaps I've been lucky. There's never been a time since I left my mother's breast, wiping my lips, that I've not looked round and immediately fallen hopelessly in love. Debt and trouble came later. I don't care. Love has been worth it.

Pray do not think that I come from a family of libertines. Libertines are usually children of the Manse. I had no such luck. I'm a child of a Session Clerk of the Free Kirk. Across the pews from me sat the Minister's daughters, Jenny and Catriona. I bowdlerise Violet Jacob's lines. When the Minister's daughters had their minds set on the ding from their feyther's iron mou, mine was set on the two lovelies sitting modestly in the Minister's family pew. I never longed for salvation in that church, only for eternal damnation at the hands of either or both of the Minister's daughters. I never had a look in.

Do thoughts like this go with a liberal upbringing? The delight in beauty has ever walked beside me. So has the love of the English language, even if I love Scots as well. Ever since I could read I had to read a chapter of the Authorised Version of the Bible every night. I've always loved that book. Its only drawback is when it gets into the wrong hands and people claim to find divine meaning in it.

There was no divine meaning in my own first book. It was *A Child's Garden of Verses*. I quote from my childhood chronicle of bedtime stories. There was no thought of Save The Children in my father's Christian household:

> The child that is not clean and neat
> With lots of toys and things to eat,
> He is a naughty child I'm sure...
> Or else his dear Papa is poor.

Be sure Nemesis knocks, even on a Presbyterian father's door.

For my first and last Hallowe'en, we had hollowed out a turnip big enough to take a candle. I was always doubtful about my father's design of the lid. It seemed to me to be ill-fitting and liable to fall in, snuffing out the light, but who was I, a five-year-old? Nor, may I explain, was I normally a dirty-tongued child, but I had learned some quaint linguistic usages from the big boys in the playground, and I was waiting for a suitable opportunity to impress my elders by their use.

Primed by Stevenson, I was taken round to the Manse to recite to the Minister. Mercifully Jenny and Catriona were elsewhere. The performance went like this:

> When I am grown to man's estate
> I shall be very proud and great.
> And not let other girls and boys
> Meddle with my toys.

At that point the top of the lantern fell in and all went dark. My time had come at last. I went off script, 'Jesus Christ, Dad,' I said, 'the fucking candle's oot!'

It was my last public performance for many years.

Ian Hamilton QC went to Glasgow University, studied law, became an advocate and has led a blameless life ever since.

Margaret Thompson Davis

The Meccano Christmas

After school, especially during the dark winter evenings, I dictated ghost stories and tales of horror to my girlfriend who was taking a secretarial course and needed practice with her shorthand. As a result I was so frightened by my imaginings I used to hare across the road from her place to my own as if all the fiends of hell were after me. We lived in the top flat then and I took the stairs three at a time and nearly battered the door down in my anxiety to get into safety.

At the time of the Empire Exhibition, an uncle and aunt came from some country area — I can't remember where — and took my brother Audley and me to the exhibition with them for a treat. Despite all my story telling — or maybe because of it — I was a timid and introverted child and when it came to sampling the thrills of the amusement park, I hung back. I was a right spoil-sport and refused to set foot on even the slowest and most harmless-looking roundabout. My wee brother had a lot more courage and eventually, thoroughly sick of me and my 'stupid carry-on', my aunt and uncle left me to my own devices and concentrated on sharing all the scream-raising amusements with Audley.

Next day at school, my classmates were eager for news of my adventures. I didn't let them down. Never, I'm sure, had they heard of such a colourful and dangerous amusement park nor anyone who showed more courage in sampling its dangers than me.

I suppose that was just an extension of the stories I used to tell to Audley and a neighbour's daughter, Esther. Sometimes, looking back, it seems that I quite often had stories thrust upon me, like the Christmas when Audley asked Santa for a Meccano set. Meccano sets were expensive. At least, they were to a family like ours. Recently a friend of mine was telling me how poor her family had been.

'Margaret,' she said in hushed tones, 'we even had frayed dinner napkins!'

I had to smile. I never even knew dinner napkins existed when I was young. Sometimes dinner didn't exist either.

My mother adored my wee brother and no wonder. He was such a lovable child with his chubby cheeks, large round eyes and breathless enthusiasms. There was never any hiding how Audley felt. He also had long thick lashes and a mop of curly hair which he said he hated because it was 'sissy'. He was an excitable and active child and he had the courage to fight against his many fears. This led him into lots of scrapes and adventures. But there were times when he could quietly become engrossed with plasticine. The stuff seemed to come to life in his hands and my mother took great pride in showing off to friends models he made.

But this Christmas he asked not for plasticine but a Meccano set. I could see, even then, how my mother could not deny him it and I'm glad she didn't. He was always a bit delicate, despite his baby plumpness. Later in his teens he became gaunt and enormous-eyed from the pain he suffered with rheumatic fever. The heart condition it left him with killed him when he was still a young man.

The rheumatic fever was the result, I'm sure, of the damp bedroom he slept in. The wallpaper used to puff darkly off the walls and every night my mother used to try to dry his blankets and mattress in front of the living-room fire. I well remember the steam rising from them.

So when Audley asked Santa for the Meccano set, my mother determined that by hook or by crook she was going to get him one. But her housekeeping had always been run on the 'rob Peter to pay Paul' method and it must have taken quite a bit of financial juggling, desperate con-tricks, and sheer nerve to get the price of one out of her pittance of housekeeping money. She managed it. Unfortunately, it meant she couldn't buy one other thing that Christmas — not even an orange for a stocking, and certainly not a present for me.

I remember how, before Christmas, she drew me aside and asked, 'Would you like half a Meccano set for Christmas, Margaret?' Knowing how Audley longed for one and sensing that it would please my mother if I said yes, I said yes.

I loved my brother and accepted without any conscious thought, and — as far as I can honestly remember — without any jealousy, that my mother loved him better than me. I never believed, in fact, that she loved me at all but I just accepted this as the normal order of things. I tried to please her though, on the off-chance that it might help. And it did please her when I said I wanted half a Meccano set for Christmas. However, at the back of my mind I still believed that Santa would bring me a doll as well.

Christmas morning came and there on the rug in front of the living-room fire (usually a black smoky fire, I remember, 'banked up with dross') sat one solitary box of Meccano. Instinctively I knew that it was vitally important for me and my lovability rating to hide my true feelings. This I managed to do. Later that day when a neighbour asked me what I'd got for Christmas, I told her in detailed and dramatic terms of how I had received a chocolate hand-bag and when I opened it there was a chocolate purse and when I opened that I found lots and lots of chocolate money inside.

I mention the incident of the Meccano Christmas, not only because of the story I told about it, but because it was a small yet important step in the development of the intuition and the need to communicate that is necessary for a novelist.

From *The Making of a Novelist*

Margaret Thomson Davis (born 1926) has published 20 novels and over 200 short stories. As well as being a member of a number of writing societies and the Scottish History Society, she is a registered lecturer in Creative Writing.

Dorothy Dunnett

❧

Great Grannies

An only child of a loving marriage never gets to hear gossip. Personally, I led a happy, peaceful existence from birth till middle age before I realised what was missing, and I have tried to make up for it ever since. Viewed from the end of the century, the events of an Edinburgh childhood spanning the years between the War to End All Wars and the next one seem both innocent and deceptive.

Take, for example, the difference between my Scottish and English grandparents. My mother's parents, born in the 1870s, were a rakish pair in Scots eyes. My grandfather Millard, pipe in mouth, nonchalantly solved the problem of travelling from Birmingham to Edinburgh by purchasing an Austin Seven motor car the size of a carton, and setting off at the wheel. He was able to steer but not to reverse; when he took a wrong turning, he and my grandmother merely got out of the car, took an end each and revolved it in the opposite direction. Or so they said.

My mother's mother (who never admitted to the ageing title of Gran) wore short skirts and lipstick, and smoked. Wonderfully, her bobbed hair never turned grey, although its chestnut colour varied occasionally. On the rare occasions we met, I found her giggly and amiable. Only later did I discover her animosity for the frozen north full of Scotsmen, one of whom had stolen her clever daughter's affections. But then, she had never been there: her roots were in Warwickshire, and my mother was a grown woman before she ever caught sight of the sea.

My Halliday grandmother wore long skirts, black button boots, and stiff-crowned hats with brims. The distance from Edinburgh to Fife being troublesome, we did not see much of her family either, but ceremonial visits were paid to their little house. She had been a professional cook, but I was never allowed (or wished) to do more in the kitchen than stand whipping cream with a fork. She was also a natural gardener, her Amon-Ras standing taller than me, big as dish-plates; her strawberries larger and darker and sweeter than anyone else's. When the village girls married, she made up the flowers for their bouquets.

Having no transport but my grandfather's bicycle, she delighted in drives in my father's cherished company Rover, and always packed food for a picnic, solemnly celebrated on the grass at the road edge, the tablecloth six inches away from the occasional wheels of passing traffic. To these occasions, she always brought a solid green football. This, tumbling from sodden baskets, bursting from shivering arm-holds was a great inconvenience, only exceeded by its cold, wet, snapping unpleasantness when cut up and eaten, which was its function.

In a tranquil, orderly life, obedient to the absolute authority of grownups, one accepted such oddities without question. It was not until I was grown that I learned more about my small, plump, warm-hearted grandma in the black-buttoned boots, who did not belong to Fife, but was the daughter of an East Lothian pit sinker. I discovered that she had fallen in love with a soldier, as my mother had, but had followed her sweetheart on a far greater journey to be married. Her wedding was held on the Rock of Gibraltar, and the first of her six children had been born on the island of Malta.

More than 60 years after that, creating the fictitious adventures of Francis Crawford of Lymond, I took my mother to the church in Valetta where my father's baptism is recorded, and then on to a picnic where, in that arid, dust-laden heat, the melting, generous sweetness of the Maltese watermelon taught us, after her death, the pleasure my grandmother always believed she was giving us.

My red-headed grandfather, son of an engineman in the Motherwell blast furnaces and another child of the Scottish industrial revolution was, naturally, a Cameron Highlander. By the time I knew him, his moustache and his crown of carefully brushed double loops of thick hair were both white, and he was the towering figure on whose knee one sat to share a poke of boiled sweeties until they were finished. (Possessed of large, square, powerful teeth, all of them sweet, the Halliday family provide diffident evidence to the fact that it is dentally possible to devour fudge, toffee and chocolate from childhood to dotage with impunity.)

Again, all was not as it seemed. Born in 1866, my Scottish grandfather left school at twelve and twice as a boy tried to run away to enrol in the army. The second time, because he was tall and well-grown, they turned a blind eye and admitted him. The name Halliday has its origins in Lowland Scotland, but it was a Highland regiment my grandfather joined, and my wedding bouquet was tied with his tartan. Where his army career took him — with his little wife and six children — I still do not fully know, although he seemed to find his experiences as a recruiting sergeant among the black houses of the Western Isles no less curious than his travels abroad. Athlete, drummer and (undoubtedly) man of decision, he ended his career as Regimental Sergeant Major, and to the end, Cameron of Lochiel was his hero.

He might have been mine (I have met a few of Lochiel's handsome descendants), but Robin Hood got in first. I won't say I didn't feel a fool, trotting out with my mother in my birthday present of hunting horn and peaked cap with a feather, but everyone seemed to know who I was. It should have taught me always to create a central character with an easily recognised logo, such as the pipe of Dixon Hawke, my next idol, a beaky detective with patent leather hair whose adventures emerged in weekly paperback pocket-books, price 6d each. Then fantasy was replaced by the inimitable experience of an Edinburgh primary and secondary school education, and hero worship (and gossip) were swept aside for twelve industrious years.

What was so memorable, or even so Scottish about that school? Not its anthem, which was *Jerusalem*, causing 1450 Scots girls regularly to belt out mellifluously someone else's hang-up about England's dark, satanic mills. Not its social standing — this was a Corporation Day School, its swarming inhabitants referred to as 'keelies' by the two élite upper bands of girls' schools in Edinburgh, and regarded darkly by the non-fee-paying band, which was spared our contributions, half obliterated by scholarships, of three guineas a year for the Infant Division, rising to £7 10s for a year at the highest level.

It was Scottish in its egalitarian attitude to those under its roof. One was aware that some girls were dark-skinned and some Jewish (and some even English) but the distinction meant nothing. Few of us ever knew what our friends' fathers did for a living and the school uniform — navy serge gym tunic over white blouse, black stockings and shoes, maroon and yellow scarf and tie, navy nap coat in winter and maroon blazer over green dress in summer — ironed out all financial distinctions.

It was of its time in its confident expectation of obedience. With 40 lassies per class, and up to five forms in a year, basic learning was inculcated by rote, and authority was as absolute as it was in our homes. No teacher, male or female, was ever addressed other than formally, whatever nicknames they might be given in private. The standard of teaching was preternaturally high (but that seemed universal) and the passing of strict term examinations led without fuss to the eventual sitting of Highers and Lowers. By that time, six different strata had been identified: two academic, dealing with classics or science, and four specialising in variations of music and art, domestic science and secretarial training. Before streaming, everyone was subjected to the same broad curriculum and I insist to my sons, when they deplore early selection, that proclivities can be discerned remarkably early. Pupils who went on to take their Mus Bachs were already hanging with flutes and cellos and fiddles at twelve. And I, at the same age, faced with 25 pieces of navy knicker to assemble and sew, knew (as did my teacher) that I could never solve the puzzle unaided.

The habit of obedience at home made discipline easy. Between the two world wars, there was a period of modest security. I know of no one in my own circle at school whose parents were separated, except by death, and those of us who are still in touch have each been married to the same person for all of our lives. Many schools still used the Lochgelly tawse, and boys could expect strappings at school and probably also at home. Because it happened everywhere, at the same accepted level, it was never questioned: who would want detention when six stingers on the palm would do instead? Girls were exempt: my ebullient, large-moustached art master used to roar his rebellion against this, begging the fates to allow him to thrash us as he thrashed the pupils in his last school. Secure, we giggled. The worst that could happen to us, apart from lines and detention, was to be singled out from our peers, to be shamed, to be subjected to sarcasm. These are harsher weapons and far more effective, but not to be used lightly. We were fortunate. We were not hurt, but we learned that words were as powerful as violence.

War burst us apart in the end. Gone were the sports days, the school dances, the myriad clubs, the operetta performances, the treats en masse to the cinema. The school closed, to allow air-raid shelters to be built, and my father's Rover, instead of taking my grandparents on picnics, took me to the echoing hall of the school where we exchanged a dozen packets of homework for a dozen set lessons, to be delivered to the homes of all those Corstorphine fellow-pupils who had not been evacuated. In the months leading up to Highers, we were taught first by remote control, and then in the school itself, breaking off during air-raid alarms, false and real, to sit in underground bunkers, singing through the programme of our last Usher Hall concert.

It was a good school, set on green meadows on the ridge of a hill overlooking the city. The meadows had once been a lake, and seagulls still frequented the trees, diving for bread cast by us and by others. One of our number made a poem about that, published in the school magazine for 1933, which I still have. In later years, I took a television crew to the spot, to film the gulls while the poem was spoken. The producer was restive: the rolling grasslands were quite bare of birds. Until I tossed up a handful of bread and a storm of white wings filled the skies, as they always did.

And the gossip? I heard none for 12 years although, as I have said, I discovered its joys later on. But then, it was being made up for us all, in a delightful way none of us could have conceived. We should not, I think, have regarded ourselves as the *crème de la crème*, even had we been whipped. But we were the happy product of a strange, small pocket in time well worth celebrating.

Dorothy Dunnett (born 1923) is a professional portrait painter and novelist. She is married to Sir Alastair Dunnett, LLD, former editor of *The Scotsman*. Lady Dunnett received an OBE in 1992 for services to literature.

Tom Fleming

❧

It's Called Growing Up

I was born into a world where horses with black plumes pulled gleaming hearses, and funerals were a thing to behold. I was born into a world where just before dusk men in flat caps climbed thin ladders to light the gas lamps, and the cure for a common cold was to stand breathing deeply beside a bubbling tar boiler in a city street. I was born into a world where the miracle of wireless was to keep silence, while the father of the house, wearing earphones, diligently poked a cat's whisker at the tiny lump of crystal contained within a compact wooden box. (All those poor cats without whiskers, I thought, and only silence for the non-grown-ups!) I was born into a midsummer morning world darkened by a total eclipse of the sun. The pleasant district of Edinburgh into which I was born was called Trinity. (When I heard the good folk in my father's church singing 'blessed Trinity', I thought they were being a little excessive in their self-satisfaction at having purchased a manse in such a desirable neighbourhood.)

My father had been born in Speyside in the January of 1873. His father, listed crofter, basket-maker, farm-servant and general labourer in three consecutive census returns, died of consumption when my father was one year old. His mother lived till she was 90. As a son of the manse, I was soon to become intimately familiar with heaven and all its joys. They were inextricably linked in my mind, from the beginning of memory, to the annual return as a family in August and early September to the places of my father's childhood. Speyside became my Paradise — and so it has remained. I was enchanted, almost from infancy, with the blue hills and the clear brown waters of river and loch, with birch and fir and rowan, with the scent of bog-myrtle, peat and heather, with the gold of harvest-fields of corn and barley. It was peopled with gods and demi-gods. The gods were mostly four-legged: Clydesdales and donkeys, collies and spaniels, squirrels and stoats. But there were whaup and pee-wee, too, and the alarm-cocks crowing from the midden at sunrise. The demi-gods were farmers and foresters, the butcher, the tailor, the baker, the cobbler with the sign in his window, BOOTS AND SHOES REPAIRED FREE OF CHARGE TOMORROW. In that Paradise country, tomorrow would never come.

One year, when I was four, my grandfather (the only one I ever knew, my mother's father) joined us in 'Paradise'. He looked for all the world like Santa Claus, with white beard and apple-rosy cheeks. He was wonderful with young children, although, like many a grandfather, he had been somewhat strict and tyrannical with his own children. My mother attended a Ladies' College in Edinburgh as a small girl, and was given the task of learning a Border Ballad by heart as part of her homework. My grandfather was brought up in Galashiels, and loved 'The Minstrelsy of the Scottish Borders'. He insisted on my mother learning her ballad in the oral tradition. At his knee parrot-fashion he taught her to say 'The Laird o' Cockpen, he's prood an' he's great...'. Next day at school she was asked to stand up and recite her ballad. With great confidence she began, 'The Laird o' Cockpen, he spewed in his grate...' — and was sent to stand outside the classroom door for unladylike behaviour!

Every morning my grandfather would take me for a walk up the Dell road into the Abernethy Forest just after breakfast. Together, old man and wee loon, we would look for 'fairy rings', circles of brightly coloured toadstools. If we were lucky enough to find one, we'd look to see if the fairies had left anything behind. They always had — plump square toffees in a golden wrapping. I came to accept it as one of the joyous 'perks' of being in Heaven. One morning I was up unusually bright and early — at least half-an-hour before breakfast. I was allowed out into the sunlit morning to play. I visited my favourite Clydesdale horse in his stable. 'Starry' was his name and he was already harnessed for the day's work. Then I inspected the hen-run and looked for eggs. And finally I walked towards the Dell road to see the foresters off to their work in the 'Nursery' beyond the high neatly-trimmed hedge. There, disappearing towards the forest, I saw the figure of my grandfather striding out, stick in one hand and in the other hand... a small white paper bag. I was about to run after him when it hit me with all the force of a divine revelation that in the small white paper bag were plump square toffees in a golden wrapping. For a moment I was devastated. No such thing as fairies? So... grown-ups tell lies? And Heaven doesn't exist? And just as suddenly I remember thinking, 'Wait a minute. This old man gets up an hour early, every morning, on holiday, to put toffees under coloured toadstools for one small boy? That can't be bad.' Tomorrows do come. It's called growing up. And heaven is not a place, or even a time. It is the realisation of an old man's secret caring. It is a small boy's dawning wonder. It is about people. It is about love.

Within four months of that holiday in Paradise my mother was dead. Before I reached my teens my father, too, had died of a broken heart at the outbreak of a second World War. He had seen one, and that was enough for any man. One year later my grandfather, with whom we'd gone to live, was also dead. I was born into a world where horses with black plumes pulled gleaming hearses and funerals were a thing to behold. Now I saw them for what they were: a part of life. The part of life that gives to every single moment its own unrepeatable sweetness.

Tom Fleming OBE (born 1927) is an actor, director and broadcaster. He was the co-founder of the Edinburgh Gateway Company, founder and first director of the Royal Lyceum Theatre Company and a former director of the Scottish Theatre Company.

Mollie Hunter

The Prize

'I want you,' said Mr Mackenzie, 'to enter for the Miller Memorial Prize.'

He was Head of English at my school. I was not yet 12 years old. And so what had it to do with me, this grand-sounding Miller Memorial Prize? I stared at him, and blurted out, 'Why, sir?'

'Because,' said Mr Mackenzie, 'I think you'll win it.'

'And what do I get if I do win?'

'Three guineas,' said he. 'All of it to spend on books of your own choice.'

Three guineas! A guinea was worth one pound and one shilling — one pound and five pence in today's money. But this was in the year 1934 when the pound was worth ten times what it is today. And I would have all that to spend on books — if he was right, that is, about my winning! 'Sir,' my voice shaking now with excitement, I asked, 'What do I have to do to enter?'

'Read this.' He thrust at me a copy of R.L. Stevenson's *Kidnapped*. 'And then write an essay about it.'

I started my reading immediately I was home from school, fell asleep that night with the book still in my hand, and took up the reading again the moment my eyes were open. I carried the book with me on my early morning paper-round, and continued reading while I went automatically through the routine of my deliveries. I read throughout all my classes in the school day that followed, read to the very last word of the story, all the while keeping the book concealed by the slightly-lifted lid of my desk. And how could I not do so?

It was only in physical terms, after all, that I was in the world of my own times. In every other sense I was in the mid-18th-century one of young David Balfour, orphaned, kidnapped aboard the ship that would have taken him to slavery in the Carolinas — if he had not met on that ship with Alan Breck Stewart, 'the man with the belt of gold', the Highlander with 'a dancing madness in his eyes'.

And such adventures as followed from that meeting — the fight when young Balfour stood shoulder to shoulder with Alan Breck in holding off the ship's crew from their murderous attempt on his gold, the shipwreck that separated the two of them, the assassination that Balfour witnessed and that was to reunite him with Alan Breck — but only as two fugitives fleeing suspected complicity in that murder!

I was there with both of them every hungry and footsore step of the way in that breathtaking sequence of 'the flight in the heather', giving thanks as often as David Balfour did for Alan Breck's skill and cunning in saving them from the pursuing soldiers, raging inwardly as Balfour so often did also against the Highlander's unshakeable conceit of himself, yet still always keenly aware of the extraordinary bond of friendship that all this was forging between these two. And when they had found safety at last, and had to part — how could they ever forget one another? How could I ever forget them?

'Never mind about the money you might win. Just write the way you feel.'

Mr Mackenzie knew how poor I was. And so that, on the day I entered for the prize, was his advice to me — unnecessary advice, as it happened, because I was not then thinking at all about the prize money. On the contrary, indeed, my whole mind was focused on the fact that I now had the chance of finding a form of words that would show how much the book had gripped me — and which would thus also be at least some sort of tribute to its author!

I wrote my essay without once lifting my head from the paper in front of me. And, as Mr Mackenzie had anticipated, I was indeed declared the winner. The three guineas of prize money — the most cash I had ever seen at one time — was eventually put into my hand. But what that meant to me was more than reward, more than just the opportunity to buy longed-for books.

That money was also the proof that I had succeeded in paying my intended tribute to R.L.S. — the great R.L.S! And although for most of my long life since then I have made my living as a writer, none of my earnings has ever given me quite the thrill of knowing how and why I had won that first three guineas.

Mollie Hunter (born 1922) is the author of 30 books. Among these are historical adventure novels for which she has been compared to R.L. Stevenson.

Geoffrey Barrow

An August Idyll

Can anyone believe that the whole month of August could go by in Argyll without a drop of rain, with the sun shining day after day often out of a cloudless sky, with the air warm and balmy? So it was in 1937, and no regurgitation of stale old meteorological records suggesting the contrary will ruffle my memory of a perfect summer.

I was 12 and ready for 'firsts'. My first sight of the Highlands, my first holiday on a farm, my first chance to climb a real hill, my first attempts to handle a rowing boat in the sea... the prospects seemed endless. Slight of build, with strong legs, skinny arms with little muscle power, eyesight whose weakness was only just beginning to show itself, a mop of sandy, almost ginger, hair and a profuse covering of freckles over face, shoulders and arms, only a year before I had nearly died of pneumonia and had been slowly nursed back to health. Now I felt ready for anything.

Imagine an old farmhouse, facing south, with its yard and steadings to the north, towards the public road. To the west, a burn rushing down from the hills and pouring into a long tidal pool which, with many interruptions of sand banks and shingle spits, joined the waters of a mile-wide sea loch. To the east, a few grass parks fringed the shore till a steep hillside pressed them, the road and a quiet little railway line into a tight space above the shore line. At this point the railway company had chosen to put a small station.

The shepherd, with grizzled hair and weather-beaten complexion, seemed to me an old man — actually Angus was probably just approaching the prime of life. He had bright blue eyes and the high cheekbones of the West Highlander. His own speech was Gaelic, but Scots was the language of the farm because the farmer himself was Scots-speaking although he had married a Gaelic-speaking Argyllswoman. The servant girl, Morag, had very little Scots or English, but she was a little simple-minded so language of any kind was not her strong point. The farm supported an orraman as well as a shepherd, a big strong fellow from the east coast who spoke with a very broad Kincardineshire accent and had a name so similar to the shepherd's that he had to be distinguished as 'the man that has a sail to his boat'. With his dinghy he used to go fishing quite often and quite successfully, and how many hours he put in for the farmer was never clear.

My father liked to fish, too, and since I wanted plenty of rowing practice we would go out on to the loch as the tide came in and while I rowed or paddled to keep the boat steady, he would fish with a rod or try his luck by trolling with a spinning lure over the stern. I was a latecomer to swimming and was still learning, capable as yet only of a rather feeble breast stroke. Life jackets or belts were unheard-of in those days, and although not one of the men on the farm would have hesitated for a moment, if required, to jump into any of the available boats and put to sea, I doubt very much if any of them could swim.

My favourite early morning walk took me on a path leading to the point where the burn flowed into the loch. On the way this path skirted a field of neeps and led past the dairy, reputedly all that remained of the old farmhouse where Scott had written *Waverley*. The first pool I reached was normally fresh water, deep and dark brown with peat yet amazingly clear, so that everything lying on the bottom was easily visible to the naked eye. At one edge of this pool a large area of the bottom was made of the purest yellow clay, easy to dig out with one's bare hands and perfect for modelling. I had a simple fore-and-aft rigged model yacht for which it was pleasant to fashion clay crewmen or cargo; thus equipped, my yacht would occupy me for many happy hours as it sailed up and down the pool. If, as often happened, it ran aground among the rocks on the far side, I had to go down to where, despite some quicksand effects, I could wade through the burn and run back upstream to retrieve it.

After my sister (a much stronger swimmer) and I had rowed right across the loch to the far side and back, I had the ambition to do this by myself. I'm not sure that my mother or father would have allowed me to go, so I took care not to ask. The boat was actually large and clumsy, and the oars were quite heavy. Although much practice had made me fairly adept at handling them, I under-estimated the oars' capacity to make my fingers stiff and sore after pulling for two miles. All the same, I managed the solo crossing and felt very pleased with myself. It's odd how the limpets and other crustacea and even the seaweed seem more interesting on the far side of a loch or bay than they are on your own side.

One Sunday morning, my sister and I came upon Angus in the yard, sweating and puffing as he held down a ewe sprawled on her back, seemingly with all kinds of revolting things wrong with her more intimate parts. Angus, his dungarees liberally smeared with grease, tar and blood, seemed unwontedly abashed. At first, we thought this had something to do with the immodesty of the situation. It was only after we had exchanged a few words that we realised Angus was deeply embarrassed at being caught in his working clothes on the Sabbath! He was either a Free Presbyterian or a Wee Free (we only half understood such distinctions), and only direst necessity would have driven him to put a beast out of her misery on the Lord's Day. As he let go of the sheep and straightened himself up, he asked us the time and exclaimed, 'Well, I must away and shift the trouser!' He later turned up spick and span for the Gaelic service at his church (a converted house) just down the road.

Made by what had quickly become 'our own burn', a glen stretched north for a mile or two, offering a choice of walks. A tributary came in half way up the glen from the west originating high up in a peat-bog by way of which one could gain access to the next glen to the north. That, in turn, led down to the coast by a route which promised wonderful views across Loch Linnhe. The road at the foot of this glen joined up with the road running past 'our' farm. Looked at on the Bartholomew's map, it seemed to my sister and me a long way — yet with plenty of sandwiches, chocolate and a bottle of water we could surely manage it. By this time, we had covered a good deal of rough ground and steep scrambles in the vicinity of the farm. We had climbed our local hill (some way short of a Munro, a phenomenon of which we had never heard), and we had even tried (in vain) to keep up with the farmer and Angus and their three collies when they gathered the sheep for the clipping. Our parents must have thought we were hardened walkers and let us go. The day was swelteringly hot, the flies were bad, the sun beat down pitilessly. But we pressed on and ate our pieces beside a little lochan hedged about with bog myrtle, heather and blaeberries. Trousers were only just beginning to come in then for teenage girls (strictly holiday wear!), and my sister wore a dark Hunting Stewart skirt which protected her legs to below the knees. Being dark anyway, she could easily bear the sun. I was reddish-haired with a fair skin and wore shorts with only ankle-length socks. I can't remember what I had on my feet, except that they were not boots and were probably not very sensible. By the time we emerged from the second glen and turned south on the coast road, my arms and legs were fairly roasted and my feet tired. As we slogged along over the last weary miles no kindly motorist offered us a lift. Would we have accepted, I wonder, or would our pride have insisted on our finishing the course?

Before we turned east for the last stretch, we passed a beautiful green island which we had already visited a few days earlier. The farmer rented the excellent grazing and had let us come with him when he and Angus and another helper took a handful of young beasts across to the island. To our surprise, the beasts were half-pulled, half-pushed into the water. As soon as it was deep enough, they were left to swim for it while one of the men held a rope — the other end had been tied into a rough halter for the animal's head. Once they reached the shore and had been freed, the heifers scampered off quite happily and were soon grazing on grass strangely greener than that on the mainland. A single family lived on the little island, speaking only Gaelic, although the husband may have had a few words of English. The children, probably just below school age, were very shy and ran about barefooted — another first for me, who had never seen this before except with very small children.

Even when you are a child, many months can go by without leaving any impression. That month of August 1937 left many impressions, sharp, deep and enduring. It also gave us quite a few expressions, many of which became embedded in the family vocabulary and have remained there ever since. One such has long been indispensable to explain something which hasn't happened, or even something which has. Either my father or my mother was expecting a package to come by rail, and we youngsters had trotted along to the station several times in vain. The stationmaster must have been fed up with the sight of us, but at least on our umpteenth visit he had the explanation: 'No, it'll not be here the day,' he said, smiling ineffably, 'there's something on the line at Crianlarich!'

Professor Geoffrey Barrow FBA **(born 1924) is a distinguished historian of medieval Scotland, who has held professorships both at St Andrews and Edinburgh Universities. He is the author of numerous volumes on the subject including** *Robert Bruce and the Community of the Realm of Scotland* **(1965) and** *The Anglo-Norman Era in Scottish History* **(1980).**

Jenny Chaplin

An Emigrant's Farewell

Emigration from our beloved homeland has long been a fact of life for Scottish families. As a wee girl growing up in Glasgow's Govan district in the 1930s, I attended many a fareweel pairty.

As a rule, these followed a set pattern which involved vast quantities of food, bottles of 'the water of life' for the adults, 'ginger' for the weans, and a wee ceilidh at which, on the command of a spun bottle, one had to do one's 'pairty piece'. And, if at all possible, the occasion had a piper, resplendent and fully kitted-out in borrowed or fifth-hand jumble-sale Hielan regalia.

Let's take a closer look at these requisite items — each important in giving a relative or dear friend a 'guid send-aff'. Incidentally, the latter phrase was that which also applied to anyone departing not for the Colonies and a new life, but for that unknown shore in the 'Land o the Leal'.

However, as to the food deemed necessary for an emigrant's fare-weel pairty, it was very similar to that which was provided for the traditional Hogmanay hooleys. There would be pancakes, sand-wiches, Empire biscuits, fly cemeteries, fern-cakes, Madeira cake, shortbread fingers, hot Scotch mutton pies, millionaire's shortbread, soda scones, and perhaps best of all, steamin slices of spice-laden, mooth-waterin clootie dumplin.

In our wee single-end, this feast of food — most of it, apart from the shop-bocht fern-cakes, home-made — would be arrayed on top of our one and only table. In honour of the occasion, this piece of furniture would be dressed overall in one of Mammy's best white bed-linen sheets. This, together with the brass candlesticks, gave it the look of a sacred shrine of some sort.

In fact, I still remember one elderly guest who, on first seeing this laden altar, found that her eyes filled with tears as she whispered in awe, 'Michty me! Ah havenae saw a spread like this since Ah buried ma puir auld man.'

Whereupon Paw, ever the accommodating host, replied, 'Weel, hen! We're hopin things'll be a wheen cheerier the nicht than a funeral tea.'

Of course, should any item of food be in short supply, then in the Scottish time-honoured tradition, Mammy would warn us, 'Noo lissen, youse lot! As far as the shop-bocht dainties goes it'll be a case o F.H.B. Mind noo — Faimly Haud Back!'

In those far-off days, bairns were brocht up tae dae whit they were telt and aye tae mind their 'Ps and Qs' when in the company of their elders and betters. Of course, as far as the delicious fern-cakes and any other such sweet-bite dainties went, then the injunction also applied tae Paw and Grandfaither. That, at least, was some small compensation.

As tae 'the water of life' for the men, the requisite bottle of sher-ry for the women and the 'ginger' for the weans, this would help kick-start the pairty. And since several of my aunties invariably declared that, 'Ah've jist tae get the smell o whisky tae be stocious' then, in no time at all, the 'wee nicht' would be in full swing. Once everybody was suitably relaxed, it would be a case of enter stage-left, Paw with an empty bottle. This he would place length-wise on the floor and having given the bottle a bit of a theatrical twirl, we would then await, with bated breath, to see 'whose turn it was tae dae a wee recitation'.

Invariably, on such nerve-shattering occasions, my own speciality would be a rendering of the poem, 'Imphm — That Awfy wurd Imphm!' This poetic gem had been written in the 1800s by my favourite Govan poet, James Nicholson, who had also been the tailor at Merryflats Workhouse (now Glasgow Southern General Hospital).

As to the other items of entertainment, Uncle Wullie always, but always, gave us a heart-breaking rendering of 'For All We Know, We May Never Meet Again'. This epic ran to about 20 verses and by the end of his recitation since it was obvious that he 'nivver spoke a mair truer wurd', there wouldnae be a dry eye in the hoose.

At this point, Grandfaither, despairing of ever getting a chance to dae his ain pairty piece, would take the law intae his ain hauns. Declaring the spinning bottle to be redundant, he would, uninvited, launch into his previously rehearsed spiel, 'The Emigrant's Fareweel Tae His Auld Granny'. Obviously this, too, had overtones of maudlin sentiment. However, since it was clearly mony a lang day since the auld yin had clapped his e'en on his ain granny, we were able to accept this tear-jerker in a lighter vein. Even so, hankies were still much in evidence as somewhat inebriated auld-stagers still let the tear doon fa.

When it was clear that the pairty spirit was about to be washed away in a flood of maudlin tears, then the 'wee nicht' would be saved by Uncle Erchie.

I suppose to the uninitiated, Uncle Erchie was yer archetypal 'wee nyaff frae Govan'. However, tae us weans, and especially when resplendent in his full, jumble-sale Hielan regalia, he was a giant among men. True, there had been one rather fraught moment when ma wee brother, Telfie, waking from a snooze, and finding himself eyeball to eyeball with Erchie's flea-bitten sporran, had thocht it tae be a monster!

However, a dawd o puff candy hastily shoved intae the tearful wean's haun soon had the pairty richt back on course. In ony case, the sound o the bagpipes being played at full-belt in the confined space of a wee single-end, would have drowned oot any ither sound known to human ken.

The fareweel pairty would end in a flood of tears, with promises of undying affection and into the laps of the emigrants, a host of gifts, otherwise known as 'wee mindins', would then be showered. That ceremony over, the pairty would break up with the guests staggerin back tae their ain but-an-bens, and the emigrants sadly back to dour contemplation of their momentous decision to quit their ain beloved Scotland.

Many a time in childhood, I had wondered what it would be like to be at the receiving end of such a shower of gifts, not to mention such a wave of tear-doon-fa emotional release.

In 1959, suddenly it was my turn to find oot...

On a raw, pea-soup foggy December nicht, my then small daughter and I set oot for Glasgow's Central Station, on the first leg of oor journey to the Cameroons in West Africa.

With typical Glesga camaraderie, the uniformed ticket collector, after eyeing our Ben Nevis of luggage, said, 'Emigratin, are youse, Hen?'

My small daughter, buoyed up with the excitement of the occasion, not to mention a fear of the unknown, piped up, 'We're going to West Africa. To meet my sailor-daddy.'

The man stopped in mid-ticket punch. Then with a raised thumb, he jerked back his official bunnet. He gave a long, low whistle. 'West Africa, did ye say, Hen? God help youse, ma wee darlin. The White Man's Grave! that's whit they cry it. The White Man's bl*** Grave!' This of course added somewhat to the heavy aura of gloom surrounding our send-aff pairty. Nor did we even have a piper to call our ain on this momentous occasion.

However, another party of fellow emigrants, obviously rather anaesthetised by some guid Scotch whisky, did have a retinue of pipers. As we watched them marching raggedly doon the length of the station platform, we were able to share in the tear-jerking strains of 'We're No Awa Tae Bide Awa'.

In that moment, overcome with emotion at parting from my beloved parents, I made a decision. In the years ahead, come what may, yes — I would 'aye come back and see ye'.

And as a hame-again Scot, now happily entrenched this past quarter of a century in the lovely Island of Bute, I am glad that I did.

For me, as for so many returned former Scots exiles, there is no happier sentiment than that expressed in the emotive words, 'East, West... Hame in Scotland's aye best.'

Previously published in *The Scots Magazine*

Jenny Chaplin (born 1928) is a Glasgow-born lecturer on creative writing whose historical and nostalgic non-fiction books sell worldwide. Her articles appear frequently in *The Scots Magazine* and in *The Highlander* (USA).

Tam Dalyell MP

My Scottish Childhood

When I was three weeks old, my mother left me, rightly in my view, to board an old Imperial Airways clipper to go with my father to Bahrain, where he was King George V's political agent. In those days of the Raj, it would have been thought strange, in the Anglo-Indian circles in which they moved and worked, if she had not put husband before infant. So I was brought up in my early years by my maternal grandmother, the no-nonsense Victorian/Edwardian Dame Mary Marjoribanks, whom I came to adore, with my grandfather, KOSB veteran of the Boer War and Gallipoli, Sir James Bruce Wilkie-Dalyell, benignly in the background.

They bred bulldogs. Nelson, Baldwin (so called because he looked like the Prime Minister, Stanley Baldwin), Shirty (as she was by name and nature), and Ruby. I remember them all as slobbering friends that kept me, an only child, company in a household of septuagenarian adults.

Albeit our house was isolated on top of a hill overlooking the Forth and the Ochils beyond, we felt totally safe. I now understand why. Whenever anybody came and looked apprehensive, as well they might, at these fearsome beasts, my grandmother would say quietly and nonchalantly, 'Don't worry, they don't go for the throat, they only go for the testicles.' Visitors visibly paled. There were, you will not be astonished to learn, no intruders. Moreover, the canine alarm system was devastatingly effective. No bulldog could slumber through the visit of a nocturnal intruder as, like the Romans on the Capitoline Hill, my grandparents kept geese as well as peafowl and hens.

My overriding memories of these early years are of the outdoors and countryside. One incident stands out particularly. When my mother returned in the autumn of 1937, she decided that she would once again keep bees for which she had been trained at the Dairy School in Kilmarnock. I was intrigued by them. I would watch these creatures for hours at a time going in and out of their hives on the business of collecting pollen and making honey.

One day, Mr Love, bee keeper of Westfield near Armadale, came to advise my mother. Between then, they dropped the excluder. The bees were angry. And if Mr Love had smoke and protective clothing, I was in shorts and a singlet. The bees took their annoyance out on me and stung me 16 times. It was sore. My mother expertly plucked out each sting — almost the first personal service she had ever done for me — telling me not to cry and that it would be good for me.

It was. So far I have not suffered from the family arthritis. I like to believe the old wife's tale that bee stings in youth prevent arthritis.

Tam Dalyell (born 1932) is the Member of Parliament for Linlithgow.

Joe Beltrami

Uniforms

I was brought up in the pits of Glasgow's 'Briggait' — Bridgegate is the correct name. This was an extremely rough area where one had to be in a position to look after oneself. My position was a difficult one because at the age of eight, my mother sent me to St Aloysius College, Garnethill. We had to wear a uniform: cap, blazer, socks and tie. So far as I can recall, I was the only person in the whole neighbourhood who had been sent to a private school requiring full uniform and regalia. Each morning I had to go to the local bakery in Parnie Street to collect rolls and milk. As I trudged this way each day, I had to pass a Teacher's bottling station in King Street where the many female assistants would shout remarks at me because of my uniform. It was like walking the gauntlet and I hated taking the route along King Street but I had no alternative. Each morning I had the same abuse rained upon me.

In particular, there was a chap called Cryans who lived in Stockwell Street and who frequently followed me when I was wearing my uniform and constantly shouted all sorts of abuse in my direction. The term 'sissy' was mild by comparison. I suffered this for about two years and tried, as best I could, to avoid this young man whose goal in life seemed to be to hurl abuse in my direction. I had never spoken to him but he used to follow me making remarks about my uniform and school bag.

After about two years I was at the end of my tether. One day, Cryans again followed me from the bus stop to my home at 132 Bridgegate. He was swearing and shouting abuse. For the first time in the previous two years I turned round and faced him. I had decided to do something about his conduct. I challenged him to go to the back-court of his address in Stockwell Street. I followed him to the back-court which was one storey up. On entering the arena I lost my temper completely and began to hammer him. He was on the ground and I continued to punch him, possibly kicked him too. I remember him saying, 'You're in earnest!' I replied, 'By God, I am.' After about ten minutes pummelling the unfortunate Cryans, who was by this time crying like a baby, a neighbour pulled me away from him and told me to go. This I did with some reluctance.

Surprisingly enough, or perhaps it's not, in the ensuing years I had no trouble whatsoever with Master Cryans, who stopped following me, stalking me. In fact, I think he avoided me from that date on, possibly in case I turned on him again.

Despite these heroics, I continued to receive the abuse of the females at the bottling plant in King Street each morning when I went for the rolls and milk. On looking back I do not know why I was able to stand up to my situation. I was clearly a fish out of water with my cap, tie, blazer and socks. The stance with Cryans was one of the few occasions when I completely lost the 'heid' and I often think of what might have happened had I not been pulled away from this horrible youth. Perhaps I have a lot to thank the neighbour for who decided to do this. As I got older, the position improved, in as much as I was not required to wear a complete uniform and could disguise myself by using an ordinary jacket without the College logo.

When I started to visit Barlinnie Prison in 1950, many of the inmates from the area knew me. On one occasion as I went towards the interview area someone shouted, 'There's fucken Laurence Dowdall.' Happily, before long this same person became a client of mine — and a staunch one at that.

On looking back, it is probably the case that the place of my upbringing was of considerable advantage to me in the long run. I knew the language and the difficulties, and the members of the criminal fraternity were not entirely foreign to me. I knew how they thought and acted. As a result, from very early on I could distinguish between 'cock and bull' rubbish and the real thing. Naivety, accordingly, was allowed to play little part in my approach to matters criminal.

One of my most vivid recollections of my childhood days was that day in early September 1939 when Britain declared war on Germany. I was all of seven years old. My mother had allowed me to walk 'round the building' which meant that I would proceed from Briggait to Stockwell Street as far as Trongate where I would negotiate a right turn into King Street and then make my way home. This was a special treat for me, particularly as I was allowed to do this on my own. When I arrived at the junction of Stockwell Street and Trongate I saw a newspaper vendor and read the billboard stating boldly: 'War declared on Germany'. I immediately looked up at the sky fully expecting to see enemy paratroopers on their way down, shortly to land in Trongate. On reflection, I must have seen newsreels of the attack on Poland or Sudetenland shortly before this. To my disappointment the sky was clear so I turned and ran home the way I had come. Hurriedly, I changed into my uniform, this time a cowboy suit, with neckerchief, sombrero hat, spurs and elaborate six-guns fitted into two handsome holsters. I sought out my short wooden rifle then left the house. I marched up Stockwell Street fully armed and prepared, as I thought, to take on the might of the German army. About an hour later, there being no apparent confrontations nor even prospects of same, I went back home just a tad frustrated. Yes, as the well-known comedian Rob Wilton used to say, 'On the day war broke out... '.

My early life did affect my position at school from time to time, albeit without my realising this to be the case. I remember treating a class-mate, Eugene Gallagher, like God Himself because he lived in Sandyhills. I had visions of hills, sandy beaches and shimmering water. I envied him immensely. After all, a visit to nearby Glasgow Green was a day out for me.

I recall my first College teacher (I was aged eight) going round the class and asking each boy what he wanted to be when he grew up. Teacher, lawyer, accountant, dentist, doctor were the replies. When it came to my turn — to the consternation of all and sundry — I replied, 'Engine driver', because my good friend who lived next door had constantly talked of being just that. After the laughter subsided, Miss Sweeney said, 'Your parents didn't send you here to be that.' I barely understood what she meant.

On thinking back, it is clear that I was so self-conscious and envious of people who lived in 'Drives' and 'Avenues' that I remember boarding a tram car in Stockwell Street (the scene of my earlier battle with Cryans) heading south. The destination was Sinclair Drive, and I sat there until the terminus was duly reached. I got out and walked the length of the drive taking in every detail of what a drive should look like. Shortly afterwards, I took another tram, this time travelling north from the same starting point. Destination: Gairbraid Avenue. The same routine was gone through — a surveillance of the immediate area. I remember not being too impressed on this occasion. That I would go to such lengths to see both a drive and an avenue must surely tell its own tale. I must have been totally overwhelmed by the desire to move from the 'Briggait' to a more pleasant-sounding address. Alas, this didn't happen until 1963 when I bought a detached villa in the pleasant-sounding Cedar Gardens, in High Burnside. I was just over 30 years old.

The 'Briggait' is now somewhat palatial by comparison with the good old days of 50-odd years ago.

Joseph Beltrami (born 1932) is a solicitor-advocate specialising in criminal law, and was the first solicitor-advocate to appear before the Criminal Appeal Court in Edinburgh. All three of his sons followed him into the law.

John Cairney

❦

From East End to West End

A thirties childhood was mostly spent outside, and for an East End Glaswegian that meant in the streets. There was plenty to do. Apart from the football, there was roller-skating on the asphalt, guidies and girds, leavie-o, kick-the-can, moshie and all the other esoteric pastimes. Everybody knew by a sort of street-osmosis when it was time to move on to the next thing. A peculiarly city game, however, if only for the boys, was what was called 'hudgies'. This was the practice of jumping on the tail of a lorry as it stopped by the traffic lights at the junction of Springfield Road and London Road. You were then carried along London Road to the next lights at Carmyle. The trick was to jump off at these lights and get a lorry back. Even if you didn't it wasn't too far to walk back. If by chance you missed the lights at Carmyle, you had another chance at Mount Vernon. After that, it was the great unknown, but that's how I got to visit Edinburgh for the first time!

I caught this lorry one afternoon at the lights on our corner. Traffic wasn't nearly as heavy then, and I had no trouble getting on the back of this big, open, empty lorry. But I missed the lights at Carmyle. What's more, I missed them at Mount Vernon, or else that lunatic driver went through a red. For he was a lunatic, or a cruel bastard. He must have seen this idiot eight-year-old clinging to his tail-board as he hurtled along the London Road. But he didn't stop. He didn't stop at Uddingston, or Newhouse, or Harthill or Bathgate, while I clung on eagerly, then anxiously, then frantically. I pulled myself up over the tail, on to the boards of the back, and crawled behind some tarpaulin to try and get some shelter from the wind as that maniac hurtled that lorry along the Edinburgh road. He didn't stop till we had reached Princes Street!

I was frozen with cold and terror as he came round and dragged me off. He was laughing his head off as he pulled me on to the pavement; taking my shoulder, he wheeled me round to face the way we had come. 'Glesca's that wey, son. Here' (he gave me threepenny bit), 'that'll get ye hauf-wey there! Unless ye want tae try an' get another hudgie back?' Still laughing, he climbed up into his cabin and drove off, leaving me tearful on the strange Edinburgh pavement.

But as I looked up I saw the castle. Wow! A real castle in a street? I was absolutely stunned. What a sight it was: Edinburgh Castle rising out of the Princes Street Gardens. It was a fantastic wonderland to a Glasgow keelie. Without hesitation, and with no thought now of my predicament, I headed straight for it. I had to get in to that place. I didn't know then that you had to go in from the Esplanade on the Royal Mile. To me the only obvious way was to climb the wall from the Gardens. In doing so, I skinned my knee badly, and lost that driver's threepenny bit. I came slowly down from the ramparts realizing that I couldn't take Edinburgh Castle all on my own. I was only eight. It started to get darker and I made my way back to Princes Street, with its foreign maroon trams. I was starving and now that all the excitement was wearing off, I suddenly became what I was — a lost and frightened little Glasgow boy all alone in Edinburgh.

I started to cry standing under the statue of a man on a horse. Nobody took the slightest notice. I tried to stop a couple of women, but they both brushed me aside. I started to howl. I must have made quite a noise for a policeman appeared and he took me along to the police box where I blubbed out my tale. A tail of a lorry ride! The Edinburgh policeman could not have been kinder. He gave me tea, and put his tunic round me while he went on the telephone. I had only a shirt and short trousers on and sannies. I was glad of the tunic. It was still warm. He then took me for a bag of chips and walked with me to the bus station while I ate them and put me on a blue bus. Then he had a word with the conductor, gave me a salute, and a bar of chocolate, and sauntered off. I gave him a wave from the platform as we drove off. The conductor let me sit at the place reserved for luggage. It was lovely and warm, and I fell asleep. It had been quite a day.

I was wakened as we were coming in to Glasgow and the conductor said, 'I wis tae let ye aff here.'

I didn't know where I was. And I got frightened again. 'But I don't live here,' I said.

'Too bad, son. But ye get aff here. They're expectin' ye.'

I was put off at Tobago Street police station, off the London Road. The bus had actually passed our own street. The conductor pointed to the door I had to go in, then the bus drove off. I went fearfully into the police station. There was a sergeant at the desk — and there was Dad in the waiting-room.

'Dad!' I flew at him, and leapt into his arms.

'Sign here, sir.' I heard the sergeant say.

From *East End To West End*

John Cairney (born 1930) is a well-loved theatre and television actor. He now lives in New Zealand.

Ronnie Corbett

The Step Rock Pierrots

Almost all my childhood holidays were spent in the Kingdom of Fife. Latterly Cellardyke, Anstruther and Crail, but perhaps for the first nine years of my life it was always St Andrews. Several families would all go for the same fortnight, and the routine never varied much day-to-day. The men would play golf over one of the three courses (the Eden, the New or the Old) in the mornings, while the children and their mums spent their time on the beach. There would be a meeting for lunch, and the whole family, weather permitting, would return to the sands — East or West — for the remainder of the day. In the evenings we would go for a walk round the Old Town, or the University, or the beach, or the countryside behind St Andrews; stop somewhere for a poke of chips and pass by the golf course to make the booking arrangements for the gentlemen for the next day.

There was at that time a fascinating group of people, The Pierrots, who entertained during the afternoons in a small open-air stadium (which could be covered at night) just by the Step Rock swimming pool. I think it was called, in the most exaggerated way, the Step Rock Pavilion, because it was hardly really properly a pavilion. However, the whole group of them entranced me, and I loved to visit the shows on the odd rather chilly afternoon. They chose to have a junior talent competition, and this was the first time I was ever to do anything in front of any number of people more than the family. I sang 'Any Umbrellas' nervously, but seemingly successfully, because I won first prize. It has always struck me as a bit strange that in St Andrews of all places my prize should take the form of a cricket bat.

So all things in my early life, and all my interests that were to come, were here encapsulated in that little holiday, and in that small 'pavilion'. My love of golf, my love of my career, and indeed a vague interest in cricket. Strange that it should all germinate in Fife.

Ronnie Corbett (born 1930) is a celebrated stage and television comedian who, with fellow comic Ronnie Barker, created the legendary *Two Ronnies* for BBC television. He also has a golf handicap of 15.

Ian Bannen

Rothesay

We spent our summer holidays in various parts of Britain but the two weeks at Easter during all my childhood and teenage years were spent at Rothesay. Since then I have travelled the world and have ridden on trams in many different countries, yet I have never forgotten the excitement, but lack the skill to put it fully into words, of the open tram from Rothesay to Ettrick Bay.

The route through Port Bannatyne didn't impress me much as a boy, but the slow climb from Port Bannatyne through the thick foliage and trees as we started to head out west, had an overpowering effect on me. I still remember every moment of the journey and will never forget it: the track continuing through the fields, the sun on the distant sea, the high mountains, the arrival at Ettrick with the sand, sea and smell of the seaweed. The bi-plane used to land there and take passengers on a flight around the bay. At the end of the day we would board the open tram, sitting with the wind whipping through between the seats, setting off again through the fields to our guest house and supper.

Then one year we arrived at Rothesay to find the open trams gone. I searched for them in the sheds but there was not a trace. My world was never the same again.

Ian Bannen is a film and television actor.

Lady Marion Fraser

❦

Memory of War at a Distance

No one in Glasgow slept much on the night of 13th March 1941. Waves of bombers, despite the best endeavours of the anti-aircraft defence, droned overhead relentlessly, heading for the vital shipyards strung out along the banks of the Clyde. When morning came, news was sparse but there was an eerie glow to the north. Rumour had it that Clydebank had taken the full force of the blitz.

The raid had lasted several hours. The all-clear siren had not sounded until the early hours of the morning so, to my unthinking delight, schools would not open at all that day. It was a lovely spring morning, the air crisp and clear. Two or three reconnaissance planes came and went, no doubt recording with satisfaction the devastation that their bombers had inflicted. We feared that their reports would encourage the bombers to return that night to finish their grisly task.

My mother was in demand as a singer at charity concerts. That evening she had an engagement in Roberton, a peaceful village on the banks of the young Clyde. To my delight it was decided that I should go with her and we were to stay overnight! I love the country and was glad to miss school. Glasgow seemed grey and grimy and people were preoccupied. Yet they were careful to shelter an eight-year-old from the tragedies and dangers of war now on our doorstep.

Lambs and daffodils greeted us when we got to Roberton on the afternoon of the 14th. After a country high tea, my mother and her friend left for their concert, leaving me in the cheerful care of the maid, neatly dressed in cap and apron. She beat me at snakes and ladders, I remember, but I was allowed to stay up late to play beside the cheerful fire.

Jen went out to bring in coal, carefully turning off the hall light before she opened the outside door. No chink of light or fire flicker must be allowed to penetrate the country blackout.

'Have you ever seen the moon rise?', she asked as she put the coal scuttle beside the hearth. 'Come and have a look.' What a romantic suggestion! I had just memorised Walter de la Mare's poem 'Silver' at school — a poem I still love. We slipped out into the porch and huddled together for warmth in the doorway. The moon in its fullest phase was rising in glorious majesty above the Culter Hills. Each feature of the valley was thrown into sharp relief, dusted with silver. The narrow river glistened as it twisted purposefully towards Lanark.

As we gazed at the moon-bewitched countryside we heard, distantly, the ominous throbbing drone of the enemy planes. A full moon made their route-finding simple. The Clyde Valley provided an easy landmark for the squadrons of bombers, flying in immaculate formation unerringly, relentlessly, towards Glasgow and the shipyards. It was a fascinating sight to watch, compelling, personally unthreatening and yet deeply disturbing. The full horrors of war had been kept from me. No television in these days brought images into our living rooms and the news management sanitised what we were told. Looking back I seem to have lived in a cocoon of unimaginative ignorance. And yet the drone of these planes flying north through the beauty of the night sky, even after 50 years, still thrums menacingly in my ears.

At last, Jen and I tired of watching. We went in to warm ourselves by the fire as she struggled to put my hair in rags, a nightly ritual to induce it to curl. Then she tucked me into bed with a 'pig' at my bedsock-clad feet and I fell asleep watching the unaccustomed dancing flames of a log fire in my bedroom.

My dad and aunt were fine when we got back the next afternoon. There had been little damage done near our home. But Mother had to go immediately to offer shelter to two refugees from the Clyde-bank blitz. They were very quiet, numb with pain from the memory of two nights of unimaginable horror. At the time, I took their silence to be sullen indifference to my childish concerns. And they didn't like my dog! I did not connect their suffering with the excitement of my evening in Roberton. All was right with my world. But we did go for tea with them when they returned to their damaged home, standing bleakly among the ruins of neighbouring tenements. Only then did I begin to understand a little of their nightmare.

Half a century on, I realise, guiltily, what a charmed and self-centred life I led. I am grateful for the gift of innocence, the security which let me live a happy childhood despite the Second World War and its dangers. Yet the evil of that night lingers in my memory. I often compare the moonlit radiance of that peaceful valley, over-flown by planes bent on the destruction and death of others, to the ugliness, brutality and heartache which afflict the lives of children caught in the grip of war at the present time. I hope that the knowledge of my insensitivity as a child can help me now to repay the legacy of my happy childhood by working to protect and rebuild blameless young lives shattered by cruel circumstance beyond their control.

Lady Marion Fraser LT, LLD (born 1932) has recently retired as Chairperson of the Board of Christian Aid for Britain and Ireland.

Annette Crosbie

Apples and Sweets

I was born in Gorebridge in 1934, and my childhood seems to have happened in another world. One with hardly any traffic, no television and a big wireless that occupied a corner of the room and was tuned and controlled by my father. Every time I hear the phrase 'surfing the Net', I think of Dad turning the dial through a bewildering cacophony of signals and sounds 'till we had to beg him to stop.

My first memory is of riding my Mickey Mouse tricycle up and down Chambers Street in Edinburgh. I was being looked after by Auntie Janie who was married to the caretaker of the Heriot-Watt College opposite the beautiful museum.

I was three when we moved to a half-finished street of little bungalows which ran parallel to the Gilmerton Road and was surrounded by fields. Most of the children were my age and there was always someone to play with. I remember walking the dog with my father in the evening 'down the burn', and spending the days playing in the woods where the burn ran.

There was a large, rather grand house in the Gilmerton Road which eventually became an outpost of the Coal Board but which in those days stood empty. We were told a lady had bought it for her son, but I don't know where that story came from and all the time the house stood there he never turned up. It had tennis courts and 'grounds'. These extended down to the burn and we could get into them from the woods. Naturally, we treated the place as a more exciting extension of our territory and what's more it had an orchard. So one evening we were hanging about at the bottom of the street with apple cores lying around us like confetti when the bobby arrived on his bike. We tried to brazen it out ('What apples?') but by the time he had promised not to tell our parents this time we were a sorry abject bunch, and I was heading for my first bout of indigestion.

The houses that were still unfinished were a wonderful playground. We scampered with casual ease across joists, and I remember using some planks as a slide and going home with my knickers stiff with splinters.

The war years hardly touched us. My dad wasn't fit enough for the services, so he banged about in the Home Guard nagging people about their blackout. I remember on cold clear nights, when my parents were seeing friends off, someone would always look up and observe 'Aye! It's a grand night for Gerry tonight!' Then you knew there would be the excitement of getting bundled into clothes over your jammies and being led across the road in the dark by the dog to the Anderson shelter built into the field for a few neighbours and us. I can still smell it: a curious mixture of damp earth, ashes and sacking.

Later, my mother got fed up with being social in the middle of the night, and we had a Morrison shelter in my parents' bedroom. This was a steel cage with a solid top that the mattress went on and when the siren sounded you dragged the bedclothes underneath. That's where my mother, the dog and I lay and listened to the planes that flew over Edinburgh to bomb Clydebank.

The intricacies of rationing. The disgusting sweets that were on sale. Every ingredient seemed to be a substitute. I think my father was in his element. He was an early pioneer of D.I.Y. and I remember the boredom of shopping with him in Woolworths, opposite what was called the North British Hotel by the Waverley Steps. He kept coming home with some new invention which was, in fact, yet another substitute. I was even subjected to something with which, it was claimed, you could fill your teeth! Presumably in case all the dentists had been called up.

For some reason my mother took me along to the Women's League of Health and Beauty somewhere in Thistle Street, I think. I can't think why. A group of us went, mums and children, in the black-out, to don our white satin tops, black satin knickers and throw ourselves into some serious physical jerks. Was this the forerunner of aerobics, I wonder? We certainly didn't need the exercise. There were very few buses and we used to walk miles up and down the Gilmerton Road to reach the trams that ran from Liberton.

This is the first time in my life that I've deliberately looked back. I'm astonished how much is there in my memory. But I'd be surprised if anyone else is interested enough to get this far and I think it's far enough.

Annette Crosbie (born 1934) is a stage, film and television actress. In 1997, she received an OBE for services to drama. She is passionately concerned about the welfare of retired racing greyhounds, of which she owns three.

Nicholas Parsons

❧

Growing Up in Glasgow

Fate was to play an unexpected part in my future… in the shape of my Uncle Hugh, my father's brother, to whom I felt very close. He asked me what I was going to do and, as I had no ideas other than acting, he made some practical suggestions. Why not become an engineer? He pointed out that I had a fine set of tools with which I was always making things, as well as repairing grandfather clocks, which had become a hobby of mine at an early age…

Uncle Hugh was a positive man, who took a personal interest. In no time, he had contacted close friends in Glasgow, who spoke on his behalf to their relations who ran a pump and turbine firm on Clydeside, Drysdale's. The next thing I knew I had been accepted for an apprenticeship by the company and was on a train to Scotland to begin a new life on my own.

During the war, travelling by train was no pleasure. There were no refreshments and strict blackout rules — dimmed lights in the carriages and blinds tightly drawn. Nor were there signs at any stations. Every signpost in the country, as well as station names, had been removed so that if the Germans landed they would have no idea where they were. I do not think the authorities had worked out that our own forces would be equally confused. Rail travel entailed shouting to anyone standing on a platform when a train stopped to establish where you were. Sometimes people refused to answer for fear you were a spy, following the slogan printed everywhere, 'Idle Talk Costs Lives'. Once the bombing started, travelling by rail became even more hazardous, as lines would be hit, and trains would be diverted or forced to a standstill if approaching a town during an air raid.

I eventually arrived in Glasgow, was met by the family friends, the McClaurens, stayed with them for the weekend in Bearsden, a very smart part of Glasgow, then was introduced to the YMCA in Sauchiehall Street, a very unsmart part of Glasgow. I found lodgings there for three guineas a week full board. The rooms were like huge, rambling dormitories, all partitioned off, with enough space for a bed and a small chest. The washing facilities were communal...

My greatest challenge came when I started work on Clydeside. Here I was, barely 16-years-old, from a well-off professional family, suddenly thrown into the rough, crude and demanding world of a Clydeside engineering yard. At first I thought everyone was speaking a different language. Their gutteral and idiosyncratic use of English, with an accent broader than the standard Glaswegian, aggressively expressed with poor diction and liberally peppered with words that I had only previously seen written on lavatory walls, took some getting used to. As I walked down Ferry Road in Yoker, wearing my newly acquired boilersuit for the first time, in the blackout one crisp January morning, I wondered if I had strayed into a foreign land. I was certainly not prepared for the work or conditions in this excellent but typical engineering yard. It was still run by the Drysdale family, even though it had recently been taken over by Weir's of Cathcart, a much bigger firm specialising in the production of pumps and turbines. What was I doing learning about these heavy machines? I was not interested in pumps. I did not even know what a turbine was until I arrived.

The firm was very kind, taking me on immediately and offering a comprehensive apprenticeship. I was to spend six months in each department, starting with the tool room, where the machine tools were forged and ground. The foreman, or gaffer, was Alec Woods, a gentle man who treated me with great tolerance. I found the hours extraordinarily demanding. I had never before stood for nearly nine hours with only one break, and my back ached. Sitting down was forbidden, except in the lunch break, and to begin with I found it so difficult that I would sneak off for a little rest where I could not be seen, sometimes to the lavatories.

We clocked on before 8 a.m. and your pay was docked for every minute you were late after 8.02. There was no such thing as a tea break. Forty-five minutes for lunch, and at 5.30 the hooter would sound to us know that we were released. Whereupon those not on overtime would stream out to catch the tram or train, or walk to their homes nearby. Eight and three-quarter hours a day, Monday to Friday, and four and a quarter hours on Saturday mornings. A 48-hour working week for which, as an apprentice, I received 9s. 7d. a week for the first months I was there — not quite 50 pence in present money.

I was a complete oddity in this environment, but if I found every-thing very strange, equally I must have appeared very strange to everyone there, with my English public-school accent and what they called 'my right proper manners'. It is perhaps one of the few things in my life of which I am proud that I was soon accepted by the other apprentices, as well as by the men. Within a short while I was known as 'Big Nick', because I was much taller than most of the apprentices, some of whom presumably had grown up undernour-ished during the Depression of the 1930s. I soon discovered that swear words were sometimes used as terms of endearment, and that it was generally a compliment when I was referred to as 'Big Nick, that English bastard'. Once again, I was being cast in the straight man role, because I could make my workmates laugh and did not take myself too seriously.

Quite early on, one of the older apprentices approached me in the direct way they spoke on any subject and enquired if I was 'a boss's man'. I asked him what he meant. He pointed out that Parsons was a famous name in turbines (which I did not know) and they all wanted to know if I was related in any way and had been sent to Drysdale's to learn my trade. I told him that there was no connection. Pleased, he said, 'That's great, because if you were a boss's man, we couldn'a talk to you. You'd be oot. But as you're not, that's fine, you're one of us.' I did not realise how flattering that was. In a working-class, passionately left-wing area that was intensely proud of its Scottish roots, I was 'one of them'. I never received any special treatment from any of the men, and certainly not the foremen. In fact, some of the foremen I had during my long apprenticeship found me difficult to handle and were probably more strict with me as a result. Most of them ruled with a fairly benevolent rod of iron. They were the boss in their own area; their word was law, and it was nothing to see one of them bawl out a young apprentice with some very choice language. If apprentices nowadays were spoken to like that, they would probably go on strike.

Something else I had to adjust to was the noise generated by the engines. It stopped only at lunchtime, and the relief was indescribable. We would hungrily devour our sandwiches (or 'pieces' as they are called, presumably because they are two pieces of bread with something in the middle) with the grimy hands that had worked the machines. Only the offices had washing facilities. They also had the canteen, which was used more by the office staff than the shop-floor workers. There was a marked division between those who wore jackets and a collar and tie and those who wore a boilersuit. The two rarely mixed. In those days, headgear was fairly traditional: nothing in the offices, peaked caps for the workers, usually a bowler hat for the foreman, and always a bowler hat for the works manager. I wore a beret, which I still have.

I soon fell into the ways of my fellow apprentices. When the hooter went at 5.30, we would run down to the main Dumbarton Road, where the trams stopped at the junction with Ferry Road. To save money, the more agile ones would jump on the back of any empty lorry travelling into central Glasgow. The technique was fairly simple: as soon as the lorry slowed at the junction, you leapt to grab a crossbar on the lorry's side or rear, swung yourself up onto the top of the panel, then slipped down on the other side. First arrivals would help latecomers as the lorry gathered speed. Sometimes there would be up to a dozen youths in the lorry, and one of them would take his cap round to collect a few coppers from the others to give to the driver.

On one occasion, I was a little later than usual in leaving. As I approached the junction I saw a lorry slowing to a halt. I ran in front of it and round to the nearside and quickly grabbed a crossbar. As I swung myself up and over, out of the corner of my eye I saw a number of lads who normally jumped the lorries. They were standing on the curbside and I wondered fleetingly why they were not jumping. A second later, I knew. I landed in a huge load of cement powder. I was covered from head to foot. I did not dare to reveal my presence to the driver, as I was now carrying some of his potential profit. At a convenient stop at some traffic lights in central Glasgow I leapt off and, looking like some ghostly apparition that had stepped out of a horror film, walked back to my lodgings, leaving pools of dust as I went.

From *The Straight Man: My Life in Comedy*

Nicholas Parsons is an actor, comedian and compere. He was host of the BBC Radio 4 show *Just a Minute* and was also rector of St Andrews University from 1988-91.

Ian Richardson

❀

Daft Wully

W hen I was a child in Edinburgh, we didn't go to the theatre at all. Every Saturday morning my sister and I would go to the Tivoli Cinema for the children's programme — ropey old westerns, an episode of Flash Gordon, a couple of Mickey Mouse cartoons and a sing-along of something like 'The red, red robin...' with a bouncing dot in lieu of a conductor.

My first theatrical experience came really quite by accident. My granny, an earthy and largely uneducated women, was a great devotee of the variety programme which played at the Palladium, the bill for which changed every few weeks and for which I think she had a season ticket. I must have been about nine when she decided to take me with her to one of these shows. I can't remember what the bill was, but there would probably have been a conjuror, somebody singing sentimental ballads, a stand-up comedian, perhaps some dancing girls. The only thing I remember was the 'dramatic interlude' which was a very truncated version of Burke and Hare with the stand-up comic playing Daft Wully, although I can't remember who the main protagonists were. I was instantly caught up in the story. My excitement grew more and more intense and when Daft Wully's body fell out of the cupboard (in this instance represented by a small curtain which would, of course, hardly have supported a body) it was all I could do not to yell out loud. This is the type of excitement that I was to try to recreate for the rest of my life, and although I have been quoted as saying that my initial urge towards acting was inspired by Laurence Olivier's *Henry V*, in truth the Burke and Hare experience was the beginning of it all. When we got home, Granny said, 'He's an awfie laddy! Just look at his tie!' We all looked at it. It was my school tie and I had chewed right through it.

Ian Richardson (born 1934) is a stage, film and television actor.

Alastair Campbell of Airds

❧

A Rare Cure for Travel Sickness

Living on the shores of Loch Fyne during the war was an idyllic upbringing. There was only one drawback. Travel to civilisation meant MacBrayne's *Loch Fyne* to Greenock or the Oban bus and, for one small boy at least, racking pangs of travel sickness which usually led to a messy and thoroughly insalubrious conclusion. There is still one stretch of the road to Oban that reminds me of its labyrinthine wanderings of the 1940s which brought its inevitable result ten minutes out of Lochgilphead, while on even the most glassy of seas there was a special smell about all MacBrayne's boats — engine oil, cooking fat, stale cigarette smoke and a whiff of disinfectant — that usually had a fatal effect.

Our most noted trip was to Buckingham Palace, no less, where King George VI was to decorate my father, on leave from the war for the event. My brother and I were clad in our best kilts for the journey and embarked on the *Loch Fyne* with great excitement. That, and the sense of occasion, even lasted during the overnight trip by sleeper from Glasgow to London where we were installed in the very smart Berkeley Hotel — where I reverted to form all over the breakfast table in front of the whole dining room.

My parents were in a dilemma, in view of the importance of the day for the family, but eventually decided I should attend the ceremony. My father disappeared to join the line of those to be decorated and, as he was the senior officer receiving the senior decoration, he was to be first in the queue. So, too, it was that my already apprehensive mother found herself with her two small boys being ushered into the front row directly under the position where the King was to stand.

There was no chance of a discreet withdrawal. My mother approached a gold-encrusted Equerry to explain the situation, and the following dialogue ensued:

'I may have to take my child out during the ceremony.'

'Quite impossible, Madam. His Majesty could not fail to notice.'

'But I may have to, if he is going to be sick again.'

'Very well, Madam, but His Majesty will have to be told... '

I do not pretend that as a cure for travel sickness this is one that is readily available, but I can vouch for its effectiveness.

Alastair Campbell of Airds (born 1937) is the Unicorn Pursuivant of Arms.

Brian Leishman

The Sea and Me

A Scottish childhood indeed. Who can forget gas lamps in the streets and steam billowing up from below and around the carriages of steam engines on a winter's evening? Yet as a Scot educated almost entirely in that country, some of my most vivid memories are those outwith Scotland. And so to sea.

I should have a great affinity with the sea given that I started very early on in life to travel upon it — not as a round-the-world yachtsman, but as a three-month-old on his way with his mother to join a father he had never seen. Sixty years ago now, and although all the memories of the many cross-equator journeys are not all that vivid now, those that are have left their mark. Not for me the luxury of flight as experienced by my nieces, their friends and others whose school holidays were spent at home just like other normal children. But what is normal? Was I not the lucky one to have had the pleasure and excitement of life on the ocean waves at such an early age? By the time I was 13, I had crossed the equator six times.

My very first crossing was not one that I can remember in any way and what my father said on meeting me for the first time is lost to history as well. I am told that we settled happily in the Argentine, moving a couple of years later across the River Plate to Uruguay — Montevideo to be precise. I suspect that the River Plate at that point might more accurately be described as more a sea than a river, and as I recall, later on I swam rather more in it than sailed upon it.

All was well in those very early days until the War. An episode close to home was the Battle of the River Plate, when the Royal Navy, in the shape of HMS *Achilles*, *Ajax* and *Exeter* intercepted and inflicted great damage on the German cruiser, the *Admiral Graf Spee*, in the area of Punta del Este (13 December 1939). This forced her into Montevideo harbour for repairs. On the 14th of that month, 61 British prisoners were released from captivity and on the 15th, the ship was scuttled by a skeleton German crew.

Shortly after the battle we returned to Scotland, my father having signed up as an expatriate volunteer. But for my sister's illness, we might well have sailed on the ship which was sunk en route with few survivors. As it was, our voyage had its full share of excitement. All adult males had to take turns on duty and had to learn how to operate the ship's somewhat indifferent and modest armament. I remember well that we all had to sleep fully dressed in case of torpedo attack and we all had a small emergency rucksack by our bunks so that no time would be lost in making for the lifeboats should the need arise. Such was the danger as we neared our destination that we found we were unable to sail up the English Channel. As a result we had to make our landfall in Ireland from whence subsequently we crossed over to Liverpool and then made our way northwards arriving in due course home to Scotland. Exciting stuff indeed, and not diminished by the passing of time.

We began the return journey to South America after the War from Southampton on the *Highland Monarch*. She had served as a troop ship during the war and was now carrying many expatriate families. This included a large contingent of West Indian soldiers who had been serving in the Middle East We picked them up in Port Said, returning them to their families in Jamaica.

Within moments of landing in Montevideo, my sister and I were whisked off for ice cream, an unheard-of luxury in wartime Scotland, but an event that brought hazy pre-war memories flooding back. Back in the sunshine, what joy to walk or cycle down to that wonderful beach of white sand and, on occasion, to the open-air pool at Pocitos, to lie in the sun and cool off in the sea. There was school, of course, but somehow the sunshine made it all seem such fun! I do recall that my first day back was quite a strain though. Although my first language had been Spanish, I had been away long enough to have forgotten it all. Happily, once learned never really forgotten and, sure enough, it soon all came back. Such hair as I have today is quite dark, but in those days my friends and I were all quite seriously bleached blond by the sun. My memories of South America are coloured totally by wonderfully sunny days and great happiness.

What happy days those were, but once again they had to come to an end as I left for school in Scotland. Now in my eleventh year, this was to be my fourth sea crossing of the equator. From sunshine and beaches, 'home' was a dramatic alternative. School was located in Kincardineshire in a setting of spectacular — nay, breathtaking — beauty, surrounded by hills and firs that engendered in me a real love for fresh air and open spaces. The fifth and sixth crossings came not long after when I was 13 and I was allowed to spend exactly one week of an eight-week summer holiday with my sister and parents in Montevideo before moving on to senior school in Edinburgh. Not for me the luxury of flying home for holidays, but rather the prospect of six weeks at sea.

On a business trip recently, with a journey which took but a matter of hours not weeks, so many memories came flooding back. Meeting up with an old friend who had joined me at school in Scotland and returned afterwards to work in the Argentine (where he lives to this day) reminded me that we don't really get old perhaps just wiser.

Major Brian Leishman (born 1936) served more than 20 years with The Cameronians (Scottish Rifles) and latterly with the King's Own Scottish Borderers before joining the staff of The Edinburgh Military Tattoo in 1977.

Eileen McCallum

❦

VJ Day

Iwoke to the sound of church bells and lay motionless under the covers. I didn't like Sundays. I had to be quiet in the morning so that Mum and Dad could have a long lie and I wasn't allowed out to play. I was wondering if there was any way I could get out of going to Sunday School (I already had a Bible for perfect attendance) when I remembered, all in a rush — it wasn't Sunday at all, it was VJ Day. I snapped my eyelids open. As far as the eye could see were books. They lined the walls, covered every flat surface and teetered in precarious piles on the floor. I slept in the wee room above the front door which had served as my father's study before my arrival and was still the repository for his ever-increasing library. Every lane in Glasgow city centre had its book barrow and Dad could no more walk past one than fly in the air. I leapt out of bed. There was no room to swing a cat — not that I would have dreamt of subjecting my darling Smuts to such an indignity. I dressed quickly: knickers, ankle socks, Clarks sandals, puff-sleeved gingham. Mum had laid my clothes out as usual over a towel rail which wobbled among the books.

I could hear the excited squeals of my friends in the back lane and bogie wheels on the cobbles. We had been collecting wood and other rubbish for weeks for the bonfire to be held tonight on the Green Hill, not very far away. We used the rough paper sacks which hung at intervals up and down the lane, each next to a piggy bin — both measures during the war to utilise household waste to the limit.

The kitchenette was filled with sunshine and Mum had the back door open, it was so warm. Smuts lay stretched out on the path. I looked past him to the back gate and saw underneath two pairs of eyes and up high, where the lattice-work began, at least another four bobbing heads. Then quick as a flash two big boys were up and over the top. 'Here, here!' said my father, who had seen it all from the breakfast table, 'What do you think you're doing?' But they were politeness itself. 'Is this where Eileen lives?' they asked, 'The wee girl that can draw?' 'Yes,' said my mother. 'We want her to draw a picture of Hirohito for the top of the bonfire.' I looked at Dad. 'OK,' he said. I tore out the middle pages of a school jotter — very carefully, you weren't supposed to — and began. The delegation waited in the back garden, Smuts peering warily from the safety of the kitchen window sill.

Someone had unlocked the back gate from the inside and a couple of my best friends were ensconced on the back doorstep, thus aligning themselves with the Talent within. I did my very best big yellow face ('Fill the space,' our art teacher said), leaving little room unfortunately for the forage cap on top, and slitty eyes. It was to be a long time before we would feel guilty at such stereotyping. I brought it to the back door, where it fluttered in the breeze while the assembled company admired it. 'We'll nail it on a big stick,' they said. 'Just a minute!' My mother grabbed the wee old cushion that Smuts slept on and gave it a shake out of the back door. 'We'll pin it on to this,' she said, 'and then it won't blow away.'

That evening we packed a flask and some jam sandwiches and made our way to the bonfire site. The streets were full of families, prams and wheelchairs, bikes whizzing in and out dangerously. The noise was the strangest thing in these little suburban streets usually so quiet of a summer evening, only a lawnmower or two moving rhythmically back and forth.

The bonfire was well underway as we approached. 'Not too near and stay where we can see you.' I found my friends and we explored the unfamiliar trees and hummocks and kicked a ball about. Grown-ups stood in groups and chatted. Laughter was everywhere, erupting joyously every few seconds. I glanced surreptitiously upwards — yes, there he was, the Emperor, like some grotesque fairy on top of a Christmas tree, swaying in the gentle breeze while the flames licked higher. I turned away to chase the ball and suddenly there was a great shout, 'There he goes!' And so he did. A shower of sparks in the darkening sky and he was history. Someone had brought a wind-up gramophone and the music began. Everyone joined in the songs that had seen them through the last six years. We had come through, although I can't honestly say I remember it as a time of trauma. I was only two in 1939. I recall hurried fumblings with the itchy navy-blue siren-suit in the middle of the night and long sessions under the dining room table, demanding 'stories' from my poor parents until the All Clear sounded. I can see Dad, with his ear to the big new wireless set, fulminating over Lord Haw-Haw's latest pronouncement. My favourite authors wrote of spies and air-raid shelters. We collected shrapnel. I had known no other childhood.

People were dancing now, hugging each other, faces red and shiny from the fire and, I realise now of course, fuelled from within as well. A neighbour who put the fear of death into us children if one of our balls landed in his precious garden, thus thoroughly embarrassing his own son, who was our friend, was singing 'Give me Five Minutes More' although the gramophone was playing 'Don't Sit Underneath the Apple Tree'. And Jessie's mum, who was always so trachled, was kicking her legs like a Bluebell girl and yes, how awful, you could just see her blue Celanese knickers. My heart went out to Jessie.

The fire was dying down now and some families headed for home. My pals and I skipped on ahead, sure-footed in the gloaming. 'Don't get lost now!'

Minutes later, tucked up in my wee room, still a glimmer of light through the curtains, I listened to Mum and Dad locking up and coming upstairs. Imagine, all of us going to bed at the same time. It had been a day full of surprises. In the small of my back, Smuts purred and clooked my old quilt with measured tread. I'd find him another cushion in the morning.

Eileen McCallum (born 1936) began her career in radio before later branching out into theatre, film and television. She is best known as Isabel Blair in Scottish Television's *High Road*.

Sir Bob Reid

❦

Be Prepared

I had lost my hand when I was nine and, while this made cricket more difficult, it didn't take much to work out that having two legs still intact made running a real possibility. When I was 12, the Highland Games were announced, and a boys' marathon (under 17s, 2 miles) intimated the opportunity was there. My father cycled and I ran. However busy he was he made time for me, and I pounded up and down the roads of Cupar. He massaged my legs and, to my brother's disgust, the bedroom reeked of wintergreen. During the week Isobel, a bonny girl with white socks, took over my father's role and became my second trainer.

As the day got nearer the excitement grew. Tactics were discussed daily and my brother took to study. A voracious reader, he turned from Dickens to Tisdall, the famous Olympic hurdler, and then finally at lunch the day before the race he pronounced. After the meat and before the pudding he produced the results of his research. A picture, a series of frightening pictures of one Dorando, the Italian marathon runner who couldn't finish on his own in the Olympics and was finally disqualified because he was helped exhausted over the line. To my mother's horror, my brother expounded the danger of marathon running, ignoring totally that the race in Cupar was two miles while in Greece it was 26 miles. My brother warned of heat and debilitation, certainly more a problem in Athens than in Cupar. However, the seed was planted.

The next day dawned and the Games began at noon. My race was at 2.30. A light lunch, in line with the Tisdall book, was the order of the day. My brother was right. By midday it was the hottest day in Scotland for 20 years. By the time I changed in the tent, the first-aid people were already in action. The race was four times around the track. The starter had 25 runners, half of them with spikes, a phenomenon I had not encountered before. The grass was rather soft and it was really hot. The starter, finding out I was twelve, began to query whether I could get the distance. I skipped past him onto the track and, looking around, there seemed to be hundreds of spectators. We were lined up and off we went.

Mindful of Dorando I settled down to what my brother described later as an unnaturally fast walking pace. But sure enough, by lap two half the field had dropped out — lying in exhausted heaps on the sides in the arms of officious first-aid men and women. By lap three, I was lapped but another eight had staggered off. I had a close look at the backs of the runners finishing first and second in front of me as they also collapsed across the line. I knew my studies stood me in good stead as I strode across the finishing tape lying broken on the ground and past the two exhausted medallists onto my last lap. As I ran on, the organisers ran out onto the track and said, 'Finish, you're third.' What effrontery! I didn't want to concede a victory. I had trained for the race and I was going to finish. Half-way round the last lap I evaded another organiser to the joy of the crowd. My Dorando preparation had left more than enough energy for me to dodge the white-coated interferers. 'We're starting the bike race, you daft little bugger.' I ran on and amid cheers I crossed the line ahead of the bikes, swerving onto the side of the track as they swept by into their second lap.

As I made my way to the tent with my brother and my white-socked trainer, I was pompously advised I had been disqualified for failing to obey instructions. My brother, as quick as a flash, defending me like some hot property, advised the official that I wasn't competing anyway because money was involved and my amateur status was paramount. The official, stunned by this immediate response, withdrew ingloriously and we left in high spirits.

Sir Bob Reid (born 1934) is the non-executive Chairman of Sears plc. He was the Chairman of the British Rail Board (1990-1995) and the first Chancellor of Robert Gordon University, Aberdeen.

Richard Wilson

❧

Don't be Stupid Boy – You Can't Speak!

The Lady Alice School, if overcrowded, was fortunate in having a purpose-built stage, complete with wings, which was regularly used by the town's amateurs, although during the day the hall served as the school's gymnasium. For those pupils who had reached eleven-plus it was considered a privilege to stay behind after school and set out rows of chairs for the performance in the evening. After tea they would return to see the show, before clearing the hall, ready for the next morning. 'And that,' says Richard, 'was my real introduction to theatre, seeing all those one-act plays performed by amateurs.' He was also fortunate in that, at that period, Scotland was rich in amateur dramatic clubs, of which there were several in Greenock, as well as drama and speech festivals.

From Lady Alice, Richard went on to the Greenock High School where he met Charlie Murray, now one of his oldest friends, whose father was headmaster at Lady Alice. Although Charlie was a year older, he had been doing a science course but decided to switch to art, which meant that he had to repeat a year, and so ended up in the same class as Richard, who was then 14 to Charlie's 15... Until then, his school chums had had games, particularly football, as their main interests, but Charlie wanted to be a painter and, indeed, went on to study at the Glasgow School of Art and became a professional... 'So Charlie was very seminal in my growing up, in that he was the first artistic person I had really known or been friendly with.'

Every summer the shipyards closed down for the first two weeks of July. The Wilsons, like many other families, took their summer holiday on the Isle of Arran. Sheets, pillow cases and everything else would be sent on ahead by railway to Ardrossan, and then transferred onto the steamer, while the family boarded a paddle steamer for the five-and-a-half hour voyage which it took in those days to reach Arran. Moira [Richard's sister] was often sick, but Richard loved to lean over the side, watching the great paddles revolving, churning the water, as the steam poured out of the funnels and the engines throbbed. It was always a great excitement to him as they neared the island and he could see the white farmhouses spread out along the small fields facing the sea, with open hillsides and stretches of moor behind and, beyond, the distant mountain peaks where once he saw the golden eagle.

On arrival at Brodick the Wilsons took a bus to Glen Sannox where 'Aunt' Peggy, as she was called, kept a small boarding house. Effie Wilson's great friend, Peggy, had married Gibbie McKinnon, a sheep farmer on Arran, a very dour man, but he and Richard's father got on well together and would spend days up on the hills tending the flocks. As soon as she saw the bus approach, 'Aunt' Peggy would come running down to the bus stop to greet them, wiping her hands on her apron. 'She seemed always to be baking,' recalls Richard.

Glen Sannox is at the foot of Goat Fell which, at 2868 feet, is the highest peak on the island. On a clear day walkers can see Argyll and Ayrshire on the mainland as well as the surrounding islands of Jura, Islay, and Mull; while to the east are the Cumbraes, Bute, the Clyde coast, with Glasgow in the far distance. Sometimes Richard would go on holiday to Arran with the Murrays and then he and Charlie would go off cycling together, pushing their bikes up the road between Lochranza and Brodick, zooming down on the other side. They also shared a passion for building dams, which continued into their teens. On one occasion, away up in the hills, miles from anywhere, they built with rocks a very elaborate dam and than, having built it, sprang it, watching the water escape with a great rush. Wet through, laughing and singing, they returned home that afternoon feeling like Viking warriors.

If Arran is rich in history with memories of Viking and other invasions, Greenock is famous for its association with Robert Burns' Highland Mary, who is supposed to have lived in Charles Street and whose remains now lie in Greenock Cemetery. Because of this association the first Burns Club, now known as the Mother Club, was founded in Greenock in 1801. Since 1986, Miss Mabel Irving has been the President of the Mother Club, the first woman to be elected to this position. She had taught English and drama at Greenock High School, and ran the school's drama society. An inspiring teacher, with a deep love of Shakespeare, she would read all the parts herself with great relish so as to bring the play alive and then get the class to read the play aloud for themselves.

One evening, when Richard was 13, he went to Mabel's house in

South Street, where she still lives, surrounded by photographs of former students and their children and grandchildren, many of whom still come to be coached by her for drama and verse speaking festivals. Richard had finally plucked up the courage to tell Mabel that he wanted to become an actor, 'and that took some doing because acting was not a profession that was encouraged in a small Scottish town like Greenock. And Mabel replied, "Don't be stupid, boy. You can't speak!" I was absolutely devastated. Mind you, she was probably quite right. I couldn't speak. I had a thick Scottish accent.'

When, a few years ago, Richard... returned to Greenock to make a short autobiographical film for BBC Scotland, he met again with his old teacher 'who seemed unchanged by the years'. She came up to him... and said, 'Iain, I didn't say you couldn't speak. I said you spoke through your teeth and, if you don't mind my saying so, you still do!'

There is no doubting that these words were deeply wounding and yet it may well have been the best thing that could have happened to him. By the time he entered the Royal Academy of Dramatic Art he had left home, travelled, seen something of the world, as well as the casualties of war, earned his living and, above all, come to know a little more about himself and about life. The initial setbacks in a career are often seen, from a later perspective, as necessary trials. Schopenhauer, in an essay, observes how, at a certain age, you look back over your life and it seems as orderly as a composed novel and, just as in Dickens' novels, little accidental meetings turn out to be the main features in the plot, so also in our lives: what seem to have been misfortunes or setbacks at the time often turn out to be critical turning points.

From James Roose-Evans, *One Foot on the Stage. The Biograpny of Richard Wilson*

Iain Carmichael (Richard) Wilson (born 1936) is a well-known actor, famous for his portrayal of Victor Meldrew in the BBC television comedy, *One Foot in the Grave*. He is also the Rector of Glasgow University.

Richard Holloway

◈

Why I Never Learnt to Play the Bagpipes

We called them picture houses, not cinemas or movie theatres; and we went to the pictures, not the movies. I use the American style now, and that's only fair for what is essentially an American medium, but I'm talking about then, not now, so I'm talking about the pictures and the picture houses that showed them. There were six in the Vale of Leven where I grew up. The Leven is the river that flows out of Loch Lomond to the Firth of Clyde at Dumbarton. Between Balloch, which sits on the south bank of the Loch, and Dumbarton five miles south-west, there are four towns — Jamestown, Alexandria, Bonhill and the Renton, which, for some reason not known to me, always takes the definite article. The whole area is an unemployment blackspot now, but in my boyhood there were dye works and textile factories along the Leven side, there were shipyards in Dumbarton and Clydebank, an hour away on the train, and the famous Singer Sewing Machine Factory at Scotstoun. I lived in Alexandria, just up the street from the railway station, and I can remember the floods of men who poured off the train at tea time every day, home from the factories and shipyards of the Leven and the Clyde. My father worked in the United Turkey Red factory in Alexandria, walking there every morning at six along the Leven side, smoking his pipe, saying nothing, coming home for his tea when we had all finished, washing at the sink in the front room of our butt and ben before eating. He was a quiet man who preferred the pub to the picture house. It was my mother who loved the pictures and took us as often as she could afford.

Alexandria had two picture houses: The Strand in Bank Street and The Hall, just opposite Bonhill Bridge. In the Renton, a couple of miles away, there was the Roxy, described by the locals as a flea pit. I don't recall going to the pictures there on my own, probably because the Renton had a reputation for tough kids and challenges to strangers. Dumbarton was different. Though it was four miles away and you had to take the bus, it was bigger and felt safer and it got newer releases. There was The Picture House just over the bridge that brought you into the town. I remember seeing Tyrone Power in *Blood and Sand* there. The La Scala was in Church Street and it did a good trade in old Westerns. The Regal was in Dumbarton East. It was on a par with the Roxy in the Renton and I only went there when I was desperate and nothing decent was showing anywhere else. But the really classy place, the star of the district, was The Rialto on College Street. To begin with, it had that exotic name. No one knew what a rialto was (no one knew what a scala was either, but it sounded commoner, somehow) and the mystery of the word added an extra promise to the fantasies it fed us.

By the middle of the '40s, I was an established film addict. As I've already said, it was my mother's fault. She took us twice a week during the war and cheered us up with Bud Abbott and Lou Costello and Bob Hope and Bing Crosby, not to mention Dorothy Lamour and that famous sarong. Even before the war I can remember being taken to the pictures, but the first film I can actually remember seeing was *Snow White and the Seven Dwarves*. I was four at the time and I laughed so hard I peed myself. 'Mammy,' I shouted, 'Mammy ahm peein masel.' Everyone took it in good part and my mother used to claim that more people laughed at me laughing at Dopey than were laughing at the actual film. It was a defining moment. I was hooked on popular culture, Hollywood style, and have remained a pushover for it ever since. Only a psychiatrist could work out the damage it has done me and I sometimes regret the time I've spent watching the back wall of Plato's cave of illusions when I could have been out in the sunshine learning Serbo-Croat or something useful, instead of giving myself up to years of escape and vicarious adventure. But a man should have the courage of his weaknesses and I only regret that I did not know soon enough that you could be paid for watching films. If I had it to do over again, I'd become a film critic rather than a bishop. I did actually try to become a bagpiper, but a certain Saturday afternoon at the Rialto put paid to that ambition.

I think it was my mother who pointed out the advertisement in the *Lennox Herald*. They were going to start a junior pipe band in the Vale. Interested children were to present themselves at Renton Primary School the following Wednesday evening. Yes, I could go and try for it. I'd always wanted to play the pipes. Right now, however, I'd better get up to Main Street to catch the bus to Dumbarton if I didn't want to miss the start of the new picture at the Rialto.

I got there just as it was starting and the usherette showed me to an outside seat next to a man sitting beside a young child. Soon I was engrossed in the film.

'It'll be getting colder soon,' the man whispered in my ear, 'you'll need a pair of gloves for the winter. Can I buy you a pair of gloves?'

Embarrassed, I muttered, 'Okay.'

'I'll need to see what size you take,' he said, taking my hand in his. 'It's very small and soft', he said.

'I need to go to the lavatory,' I whispered, as I pulled my hand away from the long pink thing that was sticking out of his trousers. I ran to the lavatory, my heart thudding, afraid he would follow. He didn't and I crept back into the audience, as far away from the man who wanted to buy me gloves as I could get. At the end of the picture, I got out before the crowd and sprinted for the bus, feeling safe only when I was on it and he wasn't. I told no one about the incident and looked forward to my first night with the pipe band.

My father took me to the Renton school the following Wednesday evening and we were led into the gym hall to sign on. As soon as I entered the room I saw him, the man from the Rialto, standing by a table, where they were taking down the names of the children to join the band. I walked out. My father was a mild man, unsurprised by anything.

'I've changed my mind,' I said, 'canny be bothered. Anyway, Uncle Harry said blowing the pipes would give me baggy cheeks.'

'Fine with me,' he said, and we walked back to Random Street.

How do children learn not to tell a soul a secret like that? I mentioned it to no one till 50 years later. It didn't stop me going to the pictures, but I never did learn to play the pipes.

The Most Reverend Richard F. Holloway (born 1933) is the Scottish Episcopal Bishop of Edinburgh.

Ronnie Browne

◈

The Trough

The horse-trough, painted racing green, a strange choice of colour for so very static an object, stood slap-bang in the middle of the triangular-shaped cobbled piece of ground at the convergence of Buccleuch Street, Chapel Street and West Crosscauseway, midway between the steepled Buccleuch and Greyfriars Free Church of Scotland and the Chapel Street Church (where there always seemed to be more weddings with 'poor-oots' than there were at its neighbour opposite). A stone's throw from the trough was the air-raid shelter — still left standing — although the war had come to an end a couple of years before.

The trough was the hub of our youthful Edinburgh empire. It was beside the trough we built the bonfire every 5th November, sitting on it to jeer at the firemen who rushed to douse the flames when the heat threatened to crack the windows of the surrounding tenements, and putting paid to any lingering thoughts of roasting tatties in the what-might-have-been red embers. The trough was the start and finish of the bike 'Le Mans' dash round the short circuit of West Crosscauseway, Nicolson Street, West Nicolson Street and back into Chapel Street. It was a convenient parking spot for the bikes after the race whilst we had a game of boules on the cobbles. The glass marbles with the twisted coloured coils in the middle made a satisfying popping noise as they dropped into their final resting places in the holes gouged out of the spaces between the 'causies'.

The cobbles made up our illicit street-football pitch. Illicit because we were engaged in a running battle with the local bobby's constant attempts to arrest our tennis ball — no such luxury as a full-sized leather one. Although in those days not nearly so much vehicular traffic plied the streets, it was obviously still dangerous to be running about dodging the few cars that were on the move. Ignoring safety considerations both for ourselves and the drivers, we would impertinently bait the police by having one of the girls posted as guard. When the man in blue was seen approaching from the direction of Parker's Stores, we would quickly pocket the ball and innocently, but insolently, stand around the trough until the bobbing helmet would disappear round the corner into Buccleuch Place, when we would shout after him, 'Polis, ye're daft!' Until, that is, the day we did just that, only for him to about-turn and come running back towards us. We took off in different directions, giggling with fright and nervous tension, some down West Cross-causeway, some up Chapel Street, and some up Quarry Close past McCallum's lemonade factory and on into the grounds of Nicolson Street Church which led out on to the safety of what we called 'The Front Street'. The giggles turned to gasps of anxiety as we found that the exits in all directions were blocked by other large blue figures in helmets, who proceeded to round us up like frightened sheep, taking names and addresses — not that we were not already known to them — and sternly admonishing with the sage warning: 'Aye, the polis are no' jist as daft as ye think. Now, bugger aff tae the Meedies an' play in safety.'

The Meedies or, as our Bruntsfield and Morningside rivals called it, The Meadows, had no great attraction for me. After all, wasn't that where the big lads played with the real ball and bullied us wee ones off the grass when we tried to play? And wasn't that where my mother had her allotment? Where there are allotments, there is work. I steered clear of the area at every opportunity, preferring the cosy familiarity of the cobbles and the trough, the scene of my first-ever sighting of an elephant, and the scene of my first-ever entre-preneurial venture.

The Empire Theatre, now known as the Festival Theatre, and des-tined in my opinion to become in itself an elephant — a great big white one — was, in my boyhood days, a thriving variety theatre in the true sense of the word. My brother and I would rush up every Saturday night to be first in the queue for the unreservable seats in 'the gods', to be joined by our mother and father just before the box-office opened. We sat enthralled watching, perhaps, the sand-dancers, Wilson Kepple and Betty, and the King of the Xylophone, the hugely rotund but amazingly nimble-fingered and fleet-of-foot Teddy King, and the first Nude Tableau, provided of course that the nudes remained absolutely static. (Why were there never any male nudes?) And all of this on the same bill. Variety, indeed. Our evening's entertainment was capped with a fish-supper from May's or Dino's chip shop in Bristo Street, eaten at home whilst being frightened to death by Valentine Dyalls' Saturday night radio ghost story, always ending with, '… and this is your story-teller… The Man in Black.'

But what of the entrepreneur and the elephant? Well, together with the variety acts staged at the Empire, from time to time the theatre would present a circus. During the run of the show, a daily procession would be seen coming up Causewayside, where the animals were stabled, passing on to Buccleuch Street at the south-east corner of The Meedies where the swingpark and the bowling greens were (and still are) up past our trough and on to the Empire. The elephants could never resist a stop at the trough. When I tell you that my mother's organic allotment leeks and rhubarb were like elephants' trunks, her cabbages and cauliflowers as big as elephants' ears, peas and beans as big as elephant's eyes, no imagination is required to know what was in the metal pails the 10-year-old entrepreneur was paid 6d (with 240 old pennies to the pound!) to fill.

**Ronnie Browne (born 1937) as one half of The Corries was a
leading proponent in the revival in Scottish folk music
which began in the 1960s.**

Bruce Lenman

Reinforced Concrete

My earliest memories are of my father going off to war in about 1942 and his decision to protect us from German bombing raids. Now that was a serious matter in Aberdeen because I can remember the raids and frightening they were. We lived near the Kittybrewster marshalling yards which is what the Germans were trying to destroy. They were phenomenally incompetent and sprayed their bombs all round. So Dad decided he'd build a shelter. We lived in a granite terraced house at 39 Hilton Street, with a sort of double granite wall between the houses. He burrowed down through the landing and staircase (we lived in the top half of the house) and excavated this incredible shelter out of reinforced concrete, like a Führer bunker, complete with bunks and air pipes and steps going up, topped by thick steel beams followed by more reinforced concrete. He absolutely loved concrete. The neighbours by this time were sending lawyer's letters about the noise and he'd forgotten to ask permission from the local authorities, which was really a bit awkward. I do remember that they sort of descended on us, and as a small boy — it must have been before I spent a year in bed with polio when I was five — I can remember the official going down with a severe look on his face and coming up holding a candle, covered in dust and looking like a ghost saying, 'Weel, ye'd need tae bla' them a' up tae get it oot, so I suppose it'll jist hae tae stay.' So that was it: the world's first nuclear shelter achieved before the atomic bomb was actually invented. And I suspect it's still there.

One of the problems was that my father, the son of a trawler skipper, was an autodidact and autodidacts have no sense of proportion. Because they think something out for themselves, it has to be right. He worked for the Forestry Commission after the war and we moved to a more select part of the town, 141 Midstocket Road, and I went to the Grammar. There he developed an obsession which required turning the parlour into a garage in this rather elegant terraced house. I remember again we had a terrible, terrible row with the neighbours and the local authority. I do remember the fire chief coming in full uniform, complete with medals and ceremonial axe, nickel-plated of course, to try to intimidate my father. The result was the most appalling row which was quite dreadful for my mother who'd already found the headlines in the local newspaper ('Local Eccentric Intends to Roll down Curtain on his Car') embarrassing. The Fire Chief stomped off in a fury leaving his axe behind him, which Dad then used to smash coal in the hope that the chief would return and demand his axe and he'd be able to pick up this battered, bent, coal-stained thing and say, 'Oh, that's what it was, was it?' But the fire chief never came back. What was absolutely maddening was that we subsequently found out that Dad had a garage (he'd bought one not far away) but he didn't have a car or even a licence. He was simply enjoying the row.

This was the sort of childhood I had. As a result, I was very good at mixing concrete and spent much of my life in Cocky Hunter's scrap yard buying scrap iron, although I did think that people looked at me strangely as I walked through the town in my overalls with large lengths of rusty iron tied to the crossbar of my bicycle. I remember passing the masters at the Grammar School who looked at me in an odd sort of way, but I didn't realise how peculiar the whole ménage appeared to the outside world. It was only later I discovered that Dad's relatives thought he was quite mad. I thought this was a normal childhood in Aberdeen.

The mania for concrete stayed with him for the rest of his life. He eventually left for London in about 1960 where quite improbably the Forestry Commission had its headquarters in Savile Row, but he actually lived in Bishops Stortford in Hertfordshire, and it was here he embarked on an enormous project building the world's biggest carport, built with his usual pattern of tall, reinforced concrete pillars with slots in the sides into which his latest passion was to slip doors with stained glass top halves: the Lenman modular building system. He was convinced this would be the pattern of the future, that people would build structures with concrete pillars and then they'd slip second-hand doors into the slots and have, for instance, an instant porch. At one stage he had something like 30 or 40 doors which he would buy for half a crown at a time from builders' yards and auction houses. He was definitely collecting them like postage stamps because my brother and I protested and he retorted that we didn't appreciate that the Art Deco ones were rare and much admired among connoisseurs. The concept that people may not actually want a carport made in a modular system which was as big as the house was not something Dad could take on board. He said, 'But they ought to. It is the cutting edge of modern life.' The next owners demolished his carport.

He did the same thing with hammocks. He came back from wartime service in the Royal Navy and told my mother that the future lay in hammocks and that houses of the future would not have beds in them at all; they'd have hooks in the walls. I remember my mother cried because she knew he wasn't joking. Now he never did this in the house, but he invented the Jack Lenman patent camping hammock which was a waterproof thing that he would carry with us instead of a tent. All you did was find two trees at a suitable distance apart and you slung your hammock between them for the night.

I was exactly eleven when we went down the Great Glen on a

camping trip. Although Dad didn't notice, because he was too pre-occupied with his new invention, I had quite acute appendicitis at this point in time and I remember the first thing that happened as we got out of the car in Inverness to start walking was that my tin mug, which was attached to my knapsack, got caught in the door and flattened. The rest of the trip sort of went like that.

The weather was unspeakably awful and we tried out the hammocks in a forest. He was a forester. The weather was horrendous — there was a slaty rock face above the wood and we could see bands of driving rain crossing it while we hung up the hammocks. Trees whip and bend in the wind, that's why they don't get uprooted. It's very important for trees to do this, but if you're in a hammock between them, you go up and down like a yo-yo: *bdoing, bdoing, bdoing*. As usual with Dad, he hadn't quite got it right. Even the waterproof lining wasn't quite waterproof. So I was sitting there, a small boy of eleven with acute appendicitis, in a non-waterproof hammock in a howling gale and driving rain in the West Highlands, going *bdoing, bdoing, bdoing*. It was the worst night of my life and I remember even I'd had enough the next day and said to him we must go into a barn. We found one of the barns that was associated with the Forestry Commission plantation and I remember crawling under some straw in it with coos immediately behind. I'd never been so happy in my life. Woke up the next morning feeling like death, and even Dad noticed that I wasn't very well. I had to be rushed to hospital and had an emergency appendectomy.

It was absolutely typical. He had worked out that this was the future, that it was workable and so it was right. Only disaster could ever persuade him that these things really weren't on. In retrospect he was an extraordinary man, though at the time, of course, none of us realized this. My brother and I thought he was a normal Scottish parent. He certainly wasn't; about that there is no doubt at all.

Bruce P. Lenman (born 1938) is the Professor of Modern History at the University of St Andrews.

Sir Bruce Pattullo

Molehills

Every April when I was very young, my mother, my sister and I went to stay with an uncle and aunt on Loch Tummelside. Strictly speaking they were not proper relations but the aunt was an old school friend of my mother's. They did not have any children of their own and since it was a hill sheep farm and it was the lambing time the 'daily routine' was wonderfully different from our home in Edinburgh.

Life in that farmhouse was always hilarious and totally unpredictable. Chaos in its nicest and funniest sense from dawn to nightfall! Sometimes real nephews and nieces were staying at the same time. All the children enjoyed the daily jobs around the farm of bringing the cows in for milking, feeding the dogs or collecting the hens' eggs, and such was the competition for the various tasks that our uncle, aunt and my mother realised they could all get some time off. League tables and a points system were drawn up and the children happily competed to do the jobs to see who could accumulate the most points! It was my first lesson in how a bit of competition can benefit everyone.

These holidays were greatly enjoyed by all until one day matters went somewhat awry. Some of the lower-lying fields by the lochside had been invaded by a colony of moles, and the gang of children were asked to flatten the molehills as one of the jobs. Unfortunately on this occasion, my uncle decided to provide a financial incentive. I cannot now be sure of the exact figure but it might have been a penny for every dozen molehills flattened. We children quickly discovered that an energetic gang could flatten a very large number of molehills in a very short period of time. At lunch time that day we reported to the adults upon the staggering success of our efforts, the enormous number of molehills flattened and with gleeful faces demanded payment of a very large sum of money. My mother was mortified at the idea that her children were seeking a financial reward bearing in mind that we were living as guests on their farm for three weeks entirely at our uncle and aunt's expense. As innocent young children we did not realise the horror of the situation that we had created as we went off with big grins and a jingle in our pockets. I never did discover how my mother resolved her embarrassment. I am sure it was sheer coincidence that 'flattening molehills' never appeared again on the list of jobs to be done.

Sir Bruce Pattullo CBE (born 1938) has spent his entire career working for the Bank of Scotland, becoming Governor of the Bank in 1991.

Jurek Pütter

❦

Bonfires

The November of 1949 had opened for business with the novel dimension of being in Primary One at the West Infant School, St Andrews. A euphoria bordering on hysteria was amplifying daily among the female staff as they prepared for the arrival of 1950. In an era still reeling under the paralysing restraints of economic austerity, caution was thrown to the wind. The 'new decade' was being heralded with an ecstasy of expression that washed through the corridors and classrooms. Square miles of paper in limitless colours and weights, textures and stiffness appeared from thin air. Pencils, crayons, chalk, paste and glue in every form, string, thin cord, rope, paints, brushes, the first felt tip pens, corrugated papers, tissue paper, coloured plasticene, stencils, transfers: a veritable cornucopia of materials all manifested themselves out of the blue.

We celebrated the forthcoming Bonfire Night in a feast of paper and silver foil flames beneath dark star-studded skies and silhouetted naked brush-like trees and angular roofs. The mania which gripped us with such intensity spilled over into our non-educational lives as we laboured to collect silver paper from cigarette packets and chocolate bars. A cosmos of stars, planets and comets with long, fiery foil tails were daily pasted onto dark blue paper fields, whilst other more complicated shapes were folded around card and suspended in their dozens from wires strung across the classroom.

Even then, as a 68-month-old scholar, I marvelled at our prodigious production. With the approach of Christmas, not only did we manufacture hundreds, if not thousands, of stars of Bethlehem, but we fabricated an Arabia of camels and vast herds of donkeys, each patiently bearing a precariously perched Madonna. Mules and asses in copious quantities were liberally distributed across the Judean hills whose slopes were accorded more than their quota of cypress trees and olive groves. And there was in our midst a modernist who daringly included a bus masquerading as a double-decker cart.

This was but a prelude to a procession of unfolding events. First, Hallowe'en came and went, wrapped up memorably in delicious menus of costume, mask and turnip-lantern making. Parties were held in homes, schools and halls. Apples and treacle scones were ceremoniously ducked for and many a brother and sister sought the opportunity to drown each other. We guised in an age when even small children could traipse the neighbourhood with safety.

The next event prematurely celebrated one-dimensionally and in joyous colour on sombre paper and within the walls of our high-ceilinged classroom was Bonfire Night. Our teacher seemed anxious to accommodate all juvenile interpretations of that unfortunate victim of judicial immolation. Our class concluded enthusiastically that he was at once androgynous, transvestite, beatified, begloved, bescarfed, behatted (several, in fact, including a pointed black witch's hat) bejacketed and becoated over a floral frock, attired with suspect wellingtons, with lipstick and moustache, cheeks suitably rouged. It satisfied everyone, having been designed by committee. I remain to this day touched by the strong image of the scarf — an oddly thoughtful gesture — a safeguard against the cold on the night of combustion.

Our neighbourhood bonfire grew vertically on a scrawny verdant triangle next to a telephone box about 200 yards from my Granny's house. To me and to scores of other budding pyromaniacs it had the splendid appearance of a potentially mobile wooden armour-plated armadillo. Vast vertical stacks of doors formed the great base, around which were placed countless rubber tyres. Within this base which soared two doors in height were placed, vertically, rolls of felt and tar roofing material. A nice touch. To this was added gloss paint of many colours. Cresting above the smooth lower walls of great girth was a veritable explosive porcupine of timber, topped triumphantly by our own classroom Guy, by now thoughtfully and decently provided with several comforting layers of underwear, both male and female, again to suit all tastes. This detail, while unseen and hidden, did not go unappreciated.

Then with unsettling suddenness, the fury of collection and construction died away. Veiled like a bride, a tarpaulin gifted for the auspicious occasion by Suttie's Lemonade Works shrouded its head and shoulders from our gaze and the elements. A hush, a lull descended and prevailed for a few days. It stood, guarded by a rota of disciples. Skies were regularly searched for rain-bearing clouds; barometers were tapped.

This was one night when darkness could not fall soon enough. In the gloom, under the illumination of non-sodium street lights, the neighbourhood proceeded in little glow-worm groups each headed by a wavering torch. The bride was unveiled to a ripple of applause. A multitude stood in worshipful expectation. The bride's wooden sides now glistened with petrol and the ladders were removed. A lone untethered rocket streaked erratically upwards, falling with an audible clatter onto roof tiles. The gloriously spectacular but tragically brief life of the pyre evolved from a few hesitant artificially-induced flames to be transformed, metamorphosing into something frighteningly and compellingly beautiful.

There was a lull before Christmas. On the last day of school of 1949, my mother and I exited the playground via the arched gateway that still miraculously survives. I bade farewell to a classroom drenched in decoration, its ceiling under stress from the gravitational pull of stars, comets, angels with and without wings, with and without heraldic trumpets, angels with golden tresses, curled and permed, or angels with no tresses at all. I returned to a house where, imaginatively, I had convinced my mother that a replica of the school's ceiling was the fashionable thing.

I come now to the last event of that decade. Anticipation of what was, after all, an adult concept was wearing thin. I had had enough of the radio and newspapers constantly exhorting listeners and readers into a glut of celebration. But something was afoot. Even in my soporific holiday stupor my father's behaviour was alarmingly friendly. Later in life I learned to read the signs better.

In the dying minutes of 1949, in a living room whose attractive ambience was underlined with a roaring coal fire and the lace-covered circular table groaned under the weight of celebration goodies, my father swept in and swept us all out into the back green. 'Behold,' he said, as he switched a row of light bulbs on, festooned along a square of washing lines, illuminating the ground carpeted with milk and lemonade bottles each bearing a firework rocket. 'Behold,' he laughed, revealing a stuffed bonfire Guy, dressed in his wartime uniform, and thoughtfully provided against the chill night air with a scarf. The Guy stood wired to a stake which grew out of a small but not insignificant bonfire. From the living room via the opened doors of the kitchen came the faint chimes of Big Ben from the radio, and then the bells of our own Town Church. He fired the bonfire, and each and every one of the rockets and prancing around and kissing and hugging us all, he yelled — all but inarticulate with laughter and holding a sherry glass — 'To the end — at last — of that stupid khaki decade.' It was ten years to the second that he had slid across the snow-covered border from occupied Poland into still neutral Hungary.

We were joined by bemused neighbours, who climbed over the fence into the garden, enjoying an unexpected bonfire. The rejoicing and fireworks continued for a long time. My aproned Granny dispensed tea, sherry, cake and shortbread to all and sundry, as well as my father's excessive production of complicated bowtie-style deep fried crusties drenched with honey and caster sugar. My mother and I sat for what seemed a long time on the roof of the old air-raid shelter. I drank my first sherry at the age of 68 months. There was even dancing that night — or was it morning? I lost track of time. A new age had begun.

Jurek Pütter (born 1944) is the son of a pre-war Polish Diplomatic Courier. He founded Grafik Orzel Design studio in 1966, Scotland's only historical research illustration establishment.

Dave Anderson

Govanhill

'If it takes a man a week to walk a fortnight, how many grapes in a barrel of tar, or would you rather have a wee bit of string?' I was five years old, for goodness sake: I wasn't ready for Surrealism. Come to think of it, maybe that's why my father called him 'Dada'.

> Here we are in Govanhill
> With Uncle Bill
> And Uncle Harry
> We're as happy as Larry
> So we are.
> Grampa plays the songs he knows
> From minstrel shows
> And G.H. Elliot
> We huvnae got a Telly — it
> docsnac matter
> Uncle Frank is a baritone
> Your Daddy is a tenor
> Harry sings like a sousaphone
> And me
> I'm no' even a fiver
>
> Grampa went to work when he was only
> twelve years old
> But the family
> Sticks together
> At the crack of dawn he went out in the
> rain and cold
> But the family
> Sticks together
> He was only seventeen when he was
> sent to war
> But the family
> Sticks together

And still he doesn't know what he was
fighting for
But the family
Sticks together
He saw Recession in the Twenties
Depression in the Thirties
And through every generation
There's been sickness and starvation
But the family sticks together
Thank god we've got each other.

It's been poverty and war and work your
life away
But the family
Sticks together
It's been wond'ring if the people will be
free someday
But the family
Sticks together
It's been struggling just to keep your wife and
kids alive
But the family
Sticks together
It's a wonder that the working people
still survive
But the family
Sticks together
From the father to the son
So the family will run
Be respectful to your mother
And protect your little brother
And the family sticks together
Thank god we've got each other

Family life
Family life
Makes all the trouble and the strife
So much easier to bear — thank god for
Family life

Meanwhile...

A' the women pitch in
Workin' in the kitchen
Makin' up the pieces for the nephews and the nieces
In nineteen-fifty
Tryin' to be happy
Washin' oot the nappies
Makin' do and mendin' a' the time it's neverendin'
Be wise be thrifty
You would think a Sunday
Ought to be the one day
You could stop the clatter take a rest an' have a natter
Wouldn't that be nifty?
It's true what they say
a woman's work is never done
In nineteen-fifty

Family life
Family life
Be a good Mother
Be a good Wife
And love the children that you bear: that's
Family life

Here ye are in Govanhill
Wi' Auntie Jill
An' Auntie Netta
You're just gonnae get a
Trolly hame
You're a right wee beauty too
It's your duty to
Grow up an' marry
Someb'dy like Uncle Harry
What a shame
Family life is the only life
It keeps a' together
You'll have weans an' you'll be a Wife
Like your Granny and your Mother

Family life
> with your brothers

Family life
> a' the others

All together
> for each other

Won't be long before it's gone
> thank god for

Family life.

**From *The Complete History of Rock'n'roll* by Dave Anderson
for Wildcat Stage Productions**

**Dave Anderson (born 1945) is a writer, performer and musical
director of Wildcat. He is probably best known for his performance as
Adam McClellen in the BBC Television sitcom *City Lights*.**

Jim McColl

The Scout Camp

Like many of my vintage, much of my social life as a youngster revolved around the Kirk and its organisations, including the Scouts. My family were long-time members of the Old High Kirk in Kilmarnock but none of us lived particularly near to it; even in my Dad's young days, his family lived at the other end of the town. We tend to think that this is a modern phenomenon! Much earlier, of course, in the late 19th century, his mother and father had lived in the parish but moved to the Bentinck to a bigger house to accommodate the growing family and to be nearer my grandfather's work in the Glenfield and Kennedy where he looked after the draught horses.

I was born and brought up in Woodstock Place (which no longer exists) as it happens, a lot nearer to the Old High but, when I reached Scout age, my Kirk didn't have a troop so I joined the 25th Ayrshire Grange Church troop, just around the corner. By the time I had reached 15 years old or thereby, a group of interested parents, including my Dad, formed a new Scout Troop at the Old High Kirk — the 29th Ayrshire — and I got a free transfer to be the first Patrol Leader. As I recall, it was definitely the Peewit patrol (no comments, please).

I am leading up to the story of a very particular summer camp, but I will keep you in suspense for a wee while longer. My Dad had two sisters and five brothers, the youngest of whom was Steve. In the late '40s, he, with my Aunt Jean and cousins Campbell and Allan, moved to the Dumfriesshire village of Moniaive. Uncle Steve became Postmaster, the Post Office being part of the wee shop he had bought. As soon as they settled, Dad and I made arrangements to visit them. I was quite excited about the trip into unknown territory because journeys to 'far off' places were still a bit of a novelty for us!

The journey proved to be quite an experience in itself because, like most families of the time, we did not own a car and therefore had to make our way by train and coach. We travelled from Kilmarnock to Thornhill by train and then boarded a bus, which awaited the arrival of the train, for the journey to Moniaive. The bus journey was, as they say in modern parlance, 'something else'.

Two things about that journey remain vivid memories to this day. First of all, the bus was a single-decker Utility bus, a term instantly recognised by those of you over 45 years of age. It was similar in outline to that famous bus driven by Richard Burton in the daring escape at the end of the film *Where Eagles Dare* (come to think of it, the journey itself was not dissimilar, but I'll come to that in a tick). It was brown and the seats were constructed of wooden slats, rather in the style of a garden bench, with no springing or cushioning. Secondly, in these days, the road from Thornhill through Penpont to Moniaive was narrow, twisting and quite hilly. It so happened that there was a young lady behind the wheel who must have had a heavy date that night because we had a coach ride worthy of a place at the Shows, a combination of the Dodgems and the Big Dipper. This was partly due to the road conditions, of course, but the activities of the driver didn't help.

At the first stop, she acquired a 'poke of chips' which she proceeded to devour with gusto, negotiating bends, hills and oncoming traffic with great panache. The evening papers, in small bundles, had to be delivered at intervals. They were in a bag by her left side — lift a bundle, transfer to the right hand, swerve across to the right side of the road and as she approached the drop zone, she prepared to throw them out the little window and return to her own side of road. The speed did not slacken one iota. Another stop and — would you believe it! — she appeared with an orange. Yes you've guessed it, as we set off again, the demoness of the transport system negotiated the next part of the journey as she peeled the orange and demolished it bit by bit. What a journey — not one for the faint-hearted.

During this delightful first visit to Moniaive, we went off to recce a potential camp site for the 29th Ayrshire Boy Scout Troop. It was a cracker of a site, on the banks of the Dalwhat Water. It had every-thing: shelter, fresh running water, woodland for picking up fuel for our campfire, flat areas for the tents, parade ground and sports, all of that about two miles from the village and surrounded by beauti-ful hilly countryside for hikes and wide games. The actual site lay in a meander of the water and seemed so self-contained, just made for the job. We reported back in due course to the Group Committee and subsequently Dad, Group Leader Bobby Osborne and Scout-master Johnny McManus paid a visit and signed up for the troop to camp there for twelve days in the summer holidays.

The date of departure arrived, we all gathered at the Kirk hall carrying wartime kit bags, some with battered old suitcases and maybe the odd Bergen, to load up the gear in a furniture wagon and then we, too, climbed up into the back for the 80-mile journey to Moniaive. Our Kirk was situated in what has become known as a 'deprived area' and none of us were particularly far-travelled, many of the lads had probably only ever got as far as the beach at Barassie, a mere twelve miles away! This was the equivalent of a trip to Disneyland nowadays.

Until we arrived at our destination, we were blissfully unaware that Moniaive was a very popular venue for Scout Troops. In our enthusiasm and naivety we could not possibly imagine that any-thing could go wrong.

As it happens, on that benign Saturday, we were the last of three troops to arrive, having had the furthest to travel. We were not taken to the same site that we had viewed in the spring. We discovered that there were three camp sites, each in a meander of the Dalwhat Water as it dropped gently down towards the village. Every prospective camper was shown the top site which was then allocated to the first to arrive! Well, we were nearest to the village!

We stayed for twelve days and had a wonderful time — the site proved all it had promised to be, we had good treks, competitions, Church Parade on the second Sunday, great grub, many badges gained. Everyone was in great fettle but as I recall, one of the Scoutmasters was having a bit of a problem with a whitlow on his finger, an important detail as you will discover.

Then, as we say in Scotland 'the chimney fell doon the lum'. We were due to travel home on the Wednesday, but on the Monday night it started to rain. Heavily. On Tuesday morning there was a council of war amongst the elders. As a result, we arranged with the farmer to have access to a vacant farm cottage on the edge of our field. Fires were lit and all inessential gear moved there ready to be loaded (dry) on the Wednesday. The rain slackened and we carried on with our programme for the day. As 'lights out' time came, the rain once again became torrential. The man with the whitlow, George, couldn't sleep, threw a few more logs on the fire, puffed another fag and tried to forget the pain — and watched as the river burst its banks and started to flood the camp site! He proved to be our early warning system.

As the water level rose, we wakened the lads and told them to dress quickly, grab their gear and head for the farm cottage — what a blessing it turned out to be. By the time I reached the last tent, the water was four inches deep, all the boys bar one were already on the move: Benny Wilson was still fast asleep and had to be tipped out of his sleeping bag!

With fires going in the cottage grates, drookit and bedraggled wee lads huddled round drinking tea and munching biscuits, chattering excitedly with that mixture of fear and excitement we have all experienced. You can imagine the babble and the noise inside, as outside our campsite gradually disappeared in a temporary loch.

Next day, the furniture wagon arrived on schedule, everything was loaded up, much of it still saturated, and then off we travelled back home. What stories there were to tell: danger, comedy, stupidity, fear, cowardice, heroics, each one putting his own slant on the events.

I suppose, if it happened today, we would be looking for someone to sue. There would be enquiries and heart searching and Scout leaders would be headlined as irresponsible and negligent. There would be oppressive new rules for Scout camps. Angry parents seeking redress! How sad. No one was hurt, no one was ever in any danger, and we all had a great story to tell. We put it down to experience.

Remind me to tell you some time the story of our camp at Balquhidder where we found the real Rob Roy cave and a company of Girl Guides from Dunblane arrived to camp in the next field. Of course, we offered to help them put their tents up...

Jim McColl MBE (born 1935), horticultural consultant and broadcaster, is a regular contributor to BBC Scotland's *Beechgrove Garden*.

Peter Morrison

Clinker Boats

My childhood was spent in Greenock, and I am glad to say I enjoyed it immensely. I hope my own children enjoyed theirs as much. I had an elder sister and younger brother. We lived in a gracious sandstone tenement on the Esplanade, with spectacular views to Rosneath and Helensburgh.

Memories of my childhood are innumerable and many concern the River, and the shipping which was in those days commonplace, from the motor torpedo boats making their way back and forward to the ordnance factory, to the Clyde steamers or the huge liners like the *Empress of Canada*. The River could be a thing of great beauty in fine weather, when the east wind blew and the clouds and rain set in, a very unwelcoming sight. At times like that the big plate glass windows in the front room rattled and the draught screen came out of the cupboard.

At the end of the Esplanade was the Royal West of Scotland Amateur Boat Club. My father (a classics master) was a member. In the fine weather, my young brother and I would pester him to 'take us out in a boat' after tea or on a weekend afternoon. If we kept on at him long enough he would always end up relenting and adrenaline levels in our house would suddenly shoot up. (I am reminded of it now when I tell my two Jack Russells they are going for a walk!) We would cycle along the Esplanade as fast as possible, with Dad pedalling sedately behind. Sometimes he walked, which was a terrible torture as we looked back along the road at his slow progress.

The Boat Club was — and still is — on the first floor, and beneath it is the shed where the boats were kept. We loved them: beautiful, big timber clinker-built boats with varnished wood and huge rowlocks and great wide seats. Some of them had ornate metal back supports in the stern.

Getting them from the shed to the water was pretty physical. They had to be manhandled onto a set of rollers and then the noisy little procession would rumble down the slipway, Dad and the Boatmaster holding the boat on either side, and the two of us darting excitedly about. A minute or two later, we would be rowing away great guns.

We loved it, although we sometimes wished it had an engine. Dad would never let us stand up — not surprisingly — as there were no life jackets and his 'not standing up' rule was the only concession to safety.

My Dad died when I was 14 and my brother was 10. When the news was broken to us, my brother, amidst our tears, said, 'We won't be able to go out in any more boats.' As it happens, I don't think we did. But about 20 years ago, I bought a boat just like the ones we used to go out in — but with an engine! It turns out that my brother did the same.

Peter Morrison's singing career took off with the BBC Television series *Songs of Scotland* in the 1970s since when he has become one of Scotland's most popular and widely-travelled ambassadors of song.

Sir Tom Farmer

Security

Thoughts of my childhood are full of good memories — memories of school, church, neighbours and, most importantly, my family. We were all true 'Leithers'. My mother and father were born there, as was my wife, Anne, who went to school with me. My grandmother and aunts lived in the same street.

I was the youngest of seven children. When asked for my childhood memories, they are of having been brought up in Leith with a feeling of complete security — security in knowing that I was surrounded by people who cared for me and everyone else in the neighbourhood. There was tremendous community spirit. As a child, I was brought up to respect other people and their property. Everybody in our neighbourhood supported each other.

But most of all there was security within the family. Being the youngest, I was spoiled and I loved it. I thought that mothers never slept. My mother was there the last thing at night and first thing in the morning when we woke up.

It is your upbringing during those early years that is so important in your development through life. I was fortunate to be born into a secure family situation in a secure neighbourhood. There can be no happier memory of childhood than that of being loved and secure, and that is certainly mine.

Sir Tom Farmer CBE KCSG **(born 1940) is Chairman and Chief Executive of Kwik-Fit Holdings plc.**

Sir Kenneth Calman

❀

From Knightswood with Love

My Scottish childhood was a happy one, though it began in the early part of the war. I remember the Anderson shelter, dug into the back lawn, and it still stands as a garden shed today. My earliest memories are from the age of three, and are of running to the shops and returning to tell the whole street that there were cream sponges at the baker's, and mince at the butcher's. In my present capacity as Chief Medical Officer to the Government, I wonder if these would be the messages I would bring back now. I can also recall as I went to the shops seeing the huge face of the Singers Clock in Dalmuir, from my home in Knightswood. I can still remember my Co-operative number: 25/1214. At about the same time, 1945, my father took me to my first football match at Ibrox. It was a classic event, Rangers versus Moscow Dynamos. The game was held up at the start when the Russians fielded twelve men. I still have the ticket as a very special memory of the event.

I have the fortunate problem of having been born on Christmas Day. The bad news is that I generally got only one present. However, the good news was that my father organised some wonderful events, and regularly hired a bus to take the family, uncles, aunts and cousins to the circus. This was all captured on 9.5mm black and white movie film, now converted to video, and is a remarkable record of the family and the local scenes.

Another unusual memory is my first contact with television. When it was introduced, we did not have one at home, but the local community centre had a 'TV Club' which, for a small membership fee, allowed the family on Sunday evenings to join a group of dedicated followers to watch *What's My Line* and the Weather Forecast. Just two hours a week of television: how things have changed!

Playing football in the street was the usual pastime after school. The goals were between two lamp-posts, the ball generally an old tennis ball, and the rules determined by the tallest and biggest. Teams, if you could call them that, were selected by the time-honoured 'one-potato, two-potato' method. Specialty games included 'Drappy' and 'Heid the Ba'. Broken windows, and I had at least one to be sorry for, were a problem. A safer pastime was to play at marbles, usually at the kerb side using the gutter as the battlefield. Cheating was frowned upon. 'Nae scheneevying' was the cry (at least that's what it sounded like), but it occurred all the same. The number of cars in the same street now would not allow the playing of such games. In the summer we would cycle to the bluebell woods, and the Girning gates, now covered by Drumchapel, and for a real adventure go along the Forth and Clyde Canal to Bowling.

My memories of my childhood would not be complete without reference to the Boys' Brigade. I was in the 237th Glasgow Company, a large one in the 1950s. It was great fun and the quality of leadership from the staff splendid. The BB display, camps in Montrose, Nairn and other places were marvellous events. We were lucky in having both a pipe and a bugle band. I played the side drum, and my brother the bagpipes. Fortunately, we had a small greenhouse for him to practise in. We both love the sound of the pipes but in a small council house it can be very loud. The BB Show, an annual event, allowed me, along with some very good friends, to publicly play the guitar in a skiffle group, sing and 'act', imitate Lonnie Donegan, and enjoy myself. What a great opportunity. The Boys' Brigade is still a remarkable movement and I'm glad to say that my wife still plays an active part in its work.

Sir Kenneth Calman (born 1941) became the first Professor of Cancer Medicine in Scotland in 1974. He moved to the Scottish Office in 1989 as Chief Medical Officer, and then in 1991 was made Chief Medical Officer to the Government.

Gus Macdonald

❦

That Sporting Life

By the time we got a telly back in 1958 I was never home to watch it. Despite having spent most of my subsequent life in broadcasting, in retrospect I am rather glad to have grown up boxless in Glasgow. It meant my childhood was dominated by sport. Even before I went to school my father was lifting me over the turnstile into Ibrox in the days when 100,000 fans squeezed in to watch Rangers. Modelling ourselves on the Willies Waddell, Woodburn or Thornton, we Tradeston boys dribbled safely down the middle of streets, which were more used by cart-horses than private cars. At night we practised keepie-up in gas-lit closes achieving a finesse with the head that was soon dispelled in Saturday morning Life Boy leagues by the sodden impact of IQ-impairing crosses which, I suspect, greatly reduced the prospects of passing your Quali. Weeknights we drilled in BB halls before vaulting and tumbling on prickly mats that would have discomfited a thick-skinned fakir.

In Scotland Street School, where the classrooms rang with metal being bashed next door in Howden's Engine Shop, 50-a-side football was played during every break. Except when the rain drove us into the playground shed. Then blood-curdling bluenose choruses would echo off the red sandstone building designed by the altogether more aesthetic Charles Rennie Mackintosh.

The football fixation was interrupted only for ritual fights among young males with a hierarchy of aggression to match that of any tribe of monkeys. The odds were tilted in my favour by a friend of my father called Johnny Kelly. He had been a corner man to Benny Lynch, the tragic little battler from next door Gorbals. Johnny gave me two sets of gloves which were said to be Benny's. One pair of puffy, heavy training gloves were laced onto spindly classmates who could then be whacked by my lighter, faster match gloves. Listening to the wireless we shadow-boxed with world champions like 'The Brown Bomber' Joe Louis and local heroes like Jackie Paterson. Coincidentally, Jackie's second was also a chum of my father, John Rafferty, who went on to become a fine sports journalist and role model for me when I worked alongside him years later on *The Scotsman*. The lore of Glasgow's boxing fancy in the '40s stretched back to bare-knuckle days and had us impressionable kids soaking our hands in salt water in imitation of John L. Sullivan who, we were assured, made himself unbeatable by pickling his fists in brine. At least it made a bag of chips taste better.

Such was my passion for sport in that dreich decade after the war I even got obsessed with cricket, listening to Test matches during the dog days of summer when the street had decamped to single rooms in Saltcoats or Ayr. Our Hutton and Compton versus Bradman and Lindwall for Australia was fought with the wicket chalked on a wall. I supported England and still do — except when they are playing Scotland. Today I am frequently surprised by the number of Scots who declare an unlikely love of cricket despite being brought up miles away from any flat green bits.

Then at Kinning Park Baths, while our mothers boiled the weekly wash in the next door steamie, endless lengths were swum despite the threat of polio from which Dr Salk subsequently saved us. We dived from high dales and even balcony banisters on the off-chance of not landing directly on one of the thrashing mass beneath. My longing for scuba diving may well be a primordial instinct to find an ecological niche not occupied by surface shoals of Glaswegian piranhas.

Roaming the back courts we constructed routes of leaps and dreeps: jumping between middens, clinging to pipes and dreeping from walls with only the occasional impalement. It helped that most railings had been melted down for the war effort. I made it to puberty with arms broken three times and only a couple of ribs cracked — the worst fall, embarrassingly, being a ten-foot plunge into the girls' outside lavatory at Scotland Street School on an over-excited leap.

We foraged to the wooded Pollok Estate in the south, raked the docks along the Clyde in search of bananas and peanuts, and marched north under the river via the Plantation tunnel as far as the Art Galleries at Kelvingrove. Much of the running I did was with bookies' lines for my father — a typical pub polymath who read the noon *Record* for racing and *Tribune* for politics. The calculation of his doubles, trebles and place bets undoubtedly helped my mental arithmetic. And without the telly there was always the Kingston Public Library which helped me get a scholarship to Allan Glen's, a fee-paying technical school which specialised in producing engineers. There I got a game of cricket on a proper pitch at last, and was also introduced to the rough pleasures of rugby which induced instant respect for the toughness of the unlikeliest toffs.

Outside school, dangerous distances were cycled to Helensburgh or across the Fenwick Moor to the Ayrshire coast, returning exhausted and increasingly fearful as the mirk came down. The derring-do self-image, with campaign medals for cycling expeditions to Torrance, Waterfoot and Lugton, was dented by having to ride a lassie's bike of the kind favoured by Janet in *Doctor Finlay's Casebook*. My mother cleaned for a minister's wife who had gifted her old bike to me, insisting that a missing crossbar mattered naught as long as the unfashionably large wheels went round. Alone among my lampless biker gang I was glad when it got dark. Fortunately a paper round covering the long avenues of Pollokshields eventually got me a turquoise Raleigh with three-speed gears to climb the hill at Shields Road which, mysteriously, now seems much less steep. Incidentally, the only Christmas tip came from the one customer who took the *Daily Record*. Every other miserly house took the Tory *Glasgow Herald* or the imperialist *Daily Express*. Little wonder that I later joined the Gorbals and Govan Young Socialists which plotted revolution in a former fruit and veg shop. It stood across the road from my home in Weir Street, just a few closes away from the old Red Clydesider, Harry McShane. Alas, Oscar Wilde was right when he said that, while socialism was a nice idea in theory, it would never catch on because it took up too many evenings. By the time Scottish Television came on air in the late '50s, my sporting enthusiasms were being displaced by nightly agitation for the class war advocated by our local barber, Harry Selby, Marxist conspirator and later MP for Govan.

One physical compensation was that the shipyard in Govan, in which I was apprenticed as a marine engineer, was like a huge adventure playground: navigating great tangles of pipe and steel mazes, balancing on planks high above engine room voids, dodging falling spanners and escaping showers of sparks. In the many idle stretches of an anarchic production process we jumped the high yard walls to play snooker in the Govan Road, sunbathed on precarious shed roofs and threw welding rods at seagulls or each other. Inter-trade lunch-time football was blind-man's buff with steel toe-caps but the yard had excellent sports grounds just up the road at

Coila Park and a Boys' Club where a former Scottish Champion, now a pattern maker, ran the boxing. I risked ostracism by leaving the markedly Protestant shipyard's football team to play for St Margaret's Boys Guild. Unfortunately, the Mags ended up beating Stephens Shipyard in a Cup Final after I scored the wining goal. Working a Sunday shift next day, my Masonic foreman warned me not to expect too much overtime in future. But it was not all sectarianism and machismo. Indeed, as energetic adolescents grew into muscled heavies, you saw how the Glasgow cult of hardness could do serious damage, and the Left always prized brain above brawn. There was even a lunchtime Philosophy Group in the yard dominated by an existentialist turner who scorned all political meetings and for obscure Sartrean reasons claimed only to go to greyhound meetings. Masochistically, I went to union meetings instead. Luckily, after a few years of joyless infighting in the recesses of Labour politics, I eventually escaped back to a sporting life of sorts and got a job in journalism.

As Scottish Television celebrates its fortieth year on air, having been so deprived of television football in my formative years, I am currently being counselled for addiction to *Scotsport* and Sky Sports. Interestingly, the only cure for this ball-watching on the box seems to be physical activity like swimming, walking up hills, and being beaten with increasing frequency by my nine-year-old grandson, Daniel, at badminton. So who knows? If I could find my old gloves, I might yet be in contention for the title of Best Fighter in the Friends of Scottish Ballet.

Gus Macdonald CBE (born 1940) went from engineering through journalism and broadcasting to become chairman of the Scottish Media Group, owners of Grampian and Scottish Television and *The Herald* and *Evening Times* newspapers.

Graeme Munro

❦

Oh, I Did Like To Be Beside the Seaside!

The seaside in the 1950s. Swan song of the Great British Summer Holiday. The end of the end of the pier. A kaleidoscope. Shake. Hundreds of elements, bright, cheerful, distinct. Shake. Another pattern. And another. Memories are like this, different facets, different lights. No single incident stands out yet the overall impression is clear and sharp. A cliché, certainly, but it seems apt. I did have a kaleidoscope, out of Miss Bailey's in the High Street.

First a holiday — Mrs Dick's guest house. Then the flitting. Just six, and moving to the seaside, 1951. End of austerity. Spreading our wings. A Victorian villa in all senses. Green dados, dark lino: the same family for 40 years. Nitromors, blow lamps, cream paint, a new time capsule.

North Berwick: population 4001 (1951 census). Who's the '1'? Me, of course. Last in! Father: 3999; Mother: 4000. Like Salman Rushdie's *Midnight's Children*, a sense of destiny? Not really. Just seemed logical at the time. The real population changed but the census figure didn't. It was in the guidebook for a decade.

North Berwick, Biarritz of the North. Mock Tudor, Scots baronial, Swiss chalet, cottage *orné*, vernacular. The harbour, the west bay (west endy) and east bay (east windy). Villas by the month for the professional classes: golf and tennis. 'Perhaps Nairn next year.' Guest houses by the fortnight: beach and putting green. 'It is nicer than Portobello.' Rooms by the week: 'Our first holiday in years.' Day trippers when heat waves struck: long queues for the SMT home. Linguistic experts could have told the season as the accents varied with the trades' holidays of Scotland.

Our home was a guest house for three months every summer. Transhumance a way of life! Pack up in May, retreat in June and recolonise in September. Summer meant freedom and excitement. Running a guest house was hard: breakfast, wash up, beds; lunch, wash up; tea, wash up; supper, wash up, set breakfast. Not much time for checking up on me: definitely an up side. Also the perks — always baking on the go, seven-pound jars of jam, ice cream in catering packs, easy to get the coupons for the special offers on the cornflake packets. Characters in the kitchen — Maria, an Austrian refugee who made Viennese pastries and taught me my first words in German; Mrs Logan who used words I had not heard before; Peggy with the terrible teeth and the heart of gold; Betty, a miner's wife from Prestonpans, who was a Catholic and cried on the Twelfth of July. Most lived on the farms and had a good command of Scots and a fund of stories. Rural depopulation was just taking off and TV only arrived in 1952.

'Changeover' Saturdays were every two weeks. Pre-credit card, most 'guests' paid in crisp £1 notes. As prices were in guineas (a built-in 5% snobbery tax) there was often change due. 'The laddie' could do quite well out of hovering in the hall when bills were settled. Half crowns, florins, shillings and sixpences: 'something for the boy to spend'. Appreciative visitors too embarrassed to tip my mother. Golden days indeed. More like 'hand your change over' days.

Two minutes to the beach. Endless opportunities. Sand castles and canal systems of labyrinthine complexity. Tunnels, dangerously, until one collapsed and the Riot Act was read. Emigration to Australia via the earth's core. Mr Auld's beach huts — a key for the season — changing without fear of dropping the towel.

Rock pools. Red sandstone, yellow wrack, green slippy, slithery slime. Limpet shells with their tenants at home: knock them off quickly or not at all. Look inside. Yuk. Then do it again, and again. No environmental education in those days! Sea anemones, jelly fish, razor shells, worm casts and mussels were our familiars.

Boats. Big ones 'always' sailed behind Craigleith, except once. I saw it. Disappointingly it didn't sink! The pilot boat, revealed after several years of malentendus to have nothing to do with pirates. The varnished wooden hull of our family yacht; only fifteen inches but still 'Clyde built'. (I say 'our' although my father did, really, buy it for me.) The boating pond on the east bay and its miniature regattas. Get the longest bamboo cane and give it a good shove. My twelfth birthday — a brown plastic Triang dinghy (six inches, but my own). Fell in three times that day and sent to bed. Not a dry eye or pair of shorts in the house! Why not a real boat, one we could sail? Why won't an orange crate float with two small boys on board? Stopped on our way to the harbour. Lucky, I suppose. And yet...

Adventures. *Famous Five*, *Secret Seven* and *Swallows and Amazons*. Acting our fantasies on the beaches, cliffs, islands and in the hinterland. The Swifts, our own version of Swallows. Tear the local map out the guidebook. Burn the edges. Made it look old. Tear a page from an exercise book and stick it on the back. Draw a club badge. A ridge tent and a meths stove. Black and pink sausages. No cups. Ever tried drinking out of half an orange skin? Camping by the sea: rabbits, primroses, cliffs, fulmars. Exploring the hinterland on foot. Terra incognita. Check the map. The tower, the windmill, the farms. Down to the Tantallon dungeon with a flickering oil lamp. Garderobes with the sea below. A terrible challenge to small boys. Irresistible really. They have electric light now and visitor facilities. Mysteries everywhere. Track down the suspects. Stake out a hotel for a whole Saturday morning. Much more fun than interactive videos. Just bring your imagination.

The Pierrots; that's what we called them. In the Harbour Pavilion. Different programme every two weeks, just like the visitors. The high point of the summer season. The jokes changed every two weeks, too. 'What's the best thing in Glasgow? The bus stop for Edinburgh!' Neatly (if predictably) reversed between the Edinburgh Trades and the Glasgow Fair. Also magicians, 'potted heid' singers, accordionists and high-kicking dancing girls. My old autograph book.

The swimming pool. Uncovered. Unheated. Canvas awnings cracking and flapping in the wind. The same pondmaster every year. Mr McCracken in white overalls, black gum boots and a black beret. Mrs McCracken likewise, but all scaled down. He gave swimming lessons ('favourable rates for local residents in September'). That was us. Even colder than August. Chittery bites earned their name. Mrs McC's thick white china mugs of Bovril — welcome heat, but nasty taste. I still can't stand Bovril. Mr McC had a long pole, a bit like the bamboo canes at the boating pond. Give you a good shove. Swim or sink.

The shops. The shopkeepers. No supermarkets. Real people, with names. Mr Gordon's and Miss Bailey's toy shops. He severe-looking, she elderly and gentle, once a Scottish swimming champion. Hampton's for sports equipment and bicycles. Danks for comics and books, one eye on the bus stop. Mr Aitken's for sweets, in big jars; cream caramels for the weekend. Chips from the 'Scotch shop' by the beach in the summer and from the 'Italian shop' in winter (followed by the spooky walk back past the old graveyard: 'whooooo, whooooo... I'm just blowing on this chip to cool it down'). Miss Bell from whom my father once memorably bought me a peach, a great luxury in those days. The Bass Rock dairy (which really was a dairy) and the Buttercup Dairy (which wasn't, but had a milkmaid and cow in tiles in the doorway). The lending library-cum-jeweller's shop with all the ticking clocks where my father got his 'whodunnits' (the only crime I can remember in 1950s North Berwick). Eels', the butcher's shop which should have been the fishmonger's. Struth's, the other butcher's with the family of pigs in the window. Mann's the cavernous ironmongers where nails were still sold by weight and you really could get everything including new wicks for the Aladdin (sadly not a magician's lamp). The nice man in the grocer's who gave me the straw that the wine bottles came in for my rabbit hutch. The West End Restaurant with its Swiss chef which served mushrooms with a mixed grill: culinary daring in 1950s North Berwick.

Personalities. Lady Screen opened fêtes but lived in a caravan with her beloved Persian dogs. Old Carl by the harbour, white beard, grey jacket, bare feet at all times and a little mongrel dog with one ear permanently up and the other down. The exotic foreign lady who was always making up her already highly made-up face in the street (tut, tut!). Kathleen, in her 40s at least but dressed like a little girl with white ankle socks; she could not speak but delivered the bread from Brodie's with a constant smile. Peter the very grumpy bus conductor from whom we used to coax sticky labels with the names of destinations. (My best was Bo'ness both far-flung and exotic with its inexplicable apostrophe.) The Burgh Surveyor, who arrived one day in righteous bureaucratic indignation, thumbs in braces, because my father had lit a bonfire without permission. Professor Richardson, antiquarian and Chief Inspector of Ancient Monuments, whose name I was to see on files 40 years later. Winston, the Border terrier.

There was a beaching of whales on the west sands. The attempted murder of a newspaper boy turned out to be a hoax. The sea was very high in 1953 at the time of the East Coast floods. The circus and 'shows' came once a year. At the time of Suez, a bi-plane flew overhead and I thought that Colonel Nasser had come to bomb North Berwick. In the height of the summer you could win £5 if you carried a *Daily Express* and could answer a simple question from their roving representative. From time to time someone local would have a letter, a recipe, or a tip published in *The Sunday Post*. A view of the harbour made the cover of the *People's Friend*. Woolworth's bought a shop in the High Street. Otherwise, great events passed us by.

North Berwick: population 4161 (1961 census). But not me. Back in Edinburgh by then. A neighbour going to Majorca. Where? Do they have the pierrots? Do they change the jokes every two weeks? Does the sun shine there? It did in North Berwick, all the time.

**Graeme Munro (born 1944) is the Director and
Chief Executive of Historic Scotland.**

Tony Roper

❧

Do It for the Boys

I sat there holding my breath. I watched her parading in front of me, teasing me mercilessly. I couldn't take my eyes off her as she strutted up and down. The excitement I felt inside was barely controllable and she knew it. The power she held over my emotions was so positive you could have charged a battery with it.

I was 15, still a school-boy and in that twilight zone of almost being a man. My voice had broken the previous summer and I now thought of girls in a strange new way that I couldn't really understand. As a boy in Glasgow growing up in the 1940s and early '50s, football was the only passion that you could admit to. Indeed, if you were informed that some young lady fancied you, that was always the signal for your pals to start hooting with uncontrollable laughter. It was definitely not kosher to admit that you even liked girls, never mind felt emotionally for one of them; if you were at an all-boys school like I was, it was considered sissy to like girls. As you got into your teens, it became totally confusing, because then it was considered sissy if you didn't like girls.

Time and again you would see some lassie that you thought was unbelievably desirable and you would be lost in thoughts of what it would be like to, well, even kiss her— never mind the full bhuna... That would be out of sight, out of this world. It was also out of the question and the only thing that teenage boys could remotely concentrate on for any length of time. First thing in the morning, constantly throughout the day and last thing at night. Then your dreams would be invaded by images of lithe young females in the recently-invented bikini, and you dreamed on top of your last dream of how it would be when you were old enough to indulge — and even wallow — in the mysterious and frighteningly exciting world of adult sexuality.

And now, in just a few moments' time, I was going to be a part of it at last. Staring at her intently, I became aware of a change in her behaviour. She no longer seemed to be so self-confident. She had turned her face towards the window and I thought I could just make out the beginnings of a tear. The light caught her eyes and made them shine even more. She looked sad. I thought that strange; why was she sad?

I know now, of course, that she was saying good-bye to innocence too, but at that moment all I could think was that at last, after years of waiting and hoping and often despairing that it would ever happen, I was going to finally know what it was like to be a real man.

Our eyes met, she smiled and it scorched my heart. My stomach churned. I was intensely concentrated and screaming silently, 'Do it. For God's sake, do it.' A barely audible sigh escaped and her lips parted. She ran her tongue over them, making them shine in the early evening sunlight. She wiped the tear from her eye, her hand reached up to the top button of her blouse and she fumbled nervously with it. My soul was crying with passion and anticipation. PLEASE, PLEASE, PLEASE. After what seemed an age, she released the top two buttons and then, oh, what bliss! She reached inside. My breath came in short gasps making my mouth dry. In a voice that was breaking with emotion, she said, 'All right, let's do it' and whipped out the whistle she kept hanging inside her blouse and blew it loud and clear. It was four o'clock and the end of the last of my school days.

Mrs. Thompson probably never knew how close she came to being hugged as I threw my school bag high up into the air.

Manhood, here I come!

Tony Roper (born 1941) is a playwright and television actor well-known from such classics as *Scotch and Wry* and *Rab C. Nesbitt*.

George Parsonage

❀

Putting Together the Pieces

Mother did a fantastic job bringing us up. How she managed with the children, the housework of such a large building, the continual secretarial work of answering phone calls, and the nursing work of undressing and looking after persons whom Father had rescued from the river, I'll never know. Father and Mother were really well-matched, not only in their love for each other and in their wish to help others, but also in their capacity for work.

Father tried hard to keep us children as far removed as possible from the sad, and often ugly, side of his work, but the extent of the family involvement was so total that this was more or less impossible. Also, Father had trained me so well that few policemen could row our boat as I could, and it was only a matter of time before I was asked to row his boat on a case. I was 15 years old. There had been a drowning accident at Bothwell Bridge, where boys playing on a raft had fallen in and one had been drowned. It was a lovely summer's day when we hitched our boat to the police van and headed into Lanarkshire.

It all seemed a great excursion at first, far removed from the grim circumstances we were involved in, as we chatted to the policemen about the day-to-day happenings; to me it was a new experience, almost a day out. We arrived at the locus and put our boat in the water. Father was told that the police had acquired the services of a sub-aqua club who had carried out a search. The police had also been dragging the river, but the body had not been found, and it was thought that it must have been swept away by the current.

I have heard from Father's friends over the years how he often did the apparently impossible, of how he succeeded when everyone else had failed, and I have now witnessed this for myself on numerous occasions, but this was the first time I saw it. After a short search in the area around the raft, the area already searched, Father recovered the boy's body. I don't really remember how I felt at that time: grief at the tragedy, seeing my first dead body, proud of my father's prowess. I don't know; one could always sense, even after years of this kind of situation, how sad Father was when he recovered a child's body, but for myself in those early years I cannot honestly state my feelings, my mind is just blank.

We prepared to return home. One of the police chiefs told Father that there had been another drowning tragedy at Motherwell, this time a boy had drowned while swimming. The policeman telephoned Motherwell and asked if they required Father's help while he was in the area, only to be told that sub-aqua units were in attendance, and Father's help would not be needed, but later in the day, the Motherwell police phoned and asked Father out. Next morning, shortly after arriving at the flat sandbanks of the Clyde at the Motherwell park, he recovered the boy's body. So much happened in those two days that I was well and truly initiated into the work of the Humane Society.

Again the Glasgow public read in the *Evening Times* of a woman being rescued on 21st May1955... As was the custom in these days, Father wore a shirt with a separate collar, using collar studs. When he entered the water to rescue this woman, the collar shrank and he very nearly choked. He had to burst the collar loose, but so bad had been the choking that the doctor had to be sent for, and Father lost his voice for fully three weeks. In fact, Mother said his voice and throat were never the same again. She backed up her statement with the fact that the sandwiches he always made with his food were only half the size they were pre-1955: as a result Father always drummed into all of us near the river not to have our ties or collars too tight, and I think he must really have got through to me to a fanatical degree, for anyone who knows me will know that it is a rare occasion to see me with my top button fastened and my tie tightened up!

I remember this rescue quite well for I was the wee boy who carried the large stretcher running as fast as I could down the river banking. When I reached the spot Father was bringing the woman round. I offered the stretcher as I had been told to do, but Father said that, since the woman was conscious, they would keep her so by walking her to the house.

Father put one of the woman's arms round his neck and another man went on the other side. This was one of my earliest recollections of this wonderful method used by Father: keep people warm, make their muscles and their brain work; in other words, make them move and try to get them talking.

The boat Father used for these rescues was a fairly new one that he had built specially for the job and was named *Bennie*.

It could be rowed double-scull without someone sitting at the back, and it would still not dive down at the bows. You could also bring a person over the side of it (most boats capsize if you try to bring people over the side). Father's boat was perfect, it went down to the water level to allow someone to be lifted, backside on the gunwale, when you'd step back and the boat would even up, you would swing the person's legs around, and they'd be in the boat. Remarkable workmanship! Every detail was worked out for perfect rowing and speed: the height of the seats, the distance from the seats to the rowlocks; open rowlocks so your oars couldn't get jammed in — you could lift it out before bringing someone aboard (you could injure someone with a fixed rowlock).

With this boat he rescued another man from the same bridge late that year. The man jumped into the river because his wife was 'nagging him'… I remember this incident well. I was a young boy helping his dad, and trying to learn (I still haven't) how to paper a room. Father was giving his bedroom a facelift. The ceiling had been painted, we had an old table in the middle of the floor, and step-ladders and basins, you will all know what it's like, and were about to put up the third or fourth roll of the new wallpaper when Father looked out of the window and saw ripples in the reflection of the McNeill Street lights on the water.

Now in those days the Clyde at night was flat calm unless a heavy west wind was blowing, and we could tell at a glance whether anything was happening on the river. Also, there were no ducks; it took us a fair amount of time and a fair number of dashes to the boats to realise that the ripples we saw in the water were usually ducks. Fortunately we learned to recognise these, but in 1957 ripples meant something in the water and that night, to Father's expert eye, they meant someone in distress.

Two or three at a time, Father jumped the 17 steps down our stairway, threw the door open and sprinted down the brae into the darkness like a greyhound off the starting grid, hurdled the fence and into the lifeboat, slipped the rope off, and his oars sped his boat to the struggling man. He lifted him into the boat and started to apply artificial respiration as the boat was spun alongside the barges.

Father and son carried the man up the brae to the house. Ann held the door open, Elizabeth was on the phone to the police, and Mother scurried around, boiling water, preparing the beds, looking out towels and hot water bottles, and generally making sure everything was in order as the patient was carried in. By now Father had brought the man round and helped him off with his wet clothes and onto the rubber bed, where he dried him then put him onto the second bed between the warm sheets and blankets, with a cup of sweet, hot tea to his lips. The police and ambulance arrived and the man was removed to the Royal Infirmary. The medical room was mopped up, the sheets on the bed changed, the wall-papering was forgotten about, for the night anyway, and a well-satisfied family settled down for tea in front of a roaring fire.

From *Rescue His Business, The Clyde His Life*

George Parsonage (born 1943) is the Officer of the Glasgow Humane Society, a unique charity founded in 1790. Following in the footsteps of his father, Benjamin Parsonage BEM, Officer 1928-79, George's work is rescue, prevention and recovery from waterways in and around the city of Glasgow.

Roddy Martine

❧

The Little Aunt

There was a blast of chill wind from the North Sea when my parents took Great-Aunt Isobel to lunch at the Marine Hotel in North Berwick. I must have been seven years old by then, and immune to the cold. I was far too excited at meeting a relative who had only been a name spoken of with affection, and in my childish preoccupation, I accidentally slammed the car door on her fingers. It must have caused her agony but, less than five foot tall and aged 80, she showed no sign of pain, only concern over my embarrassment.

Children have no great understanding of continuity, and whereas then I was aware only of looking upon Great-Aunt Isobel as a curiosity, I realise now she must have subjected me to a far more poignant scrutiny. For while there was nothing she did not know about me, even to this day I know very little about her. My recollection is of a frail old lady wrapped up against the cold, but thrilled at a day's outing. It was to be years before I began to find out anything more about her, and by then it was almost too late. There was nobody left to remember anything other than the fact that she had once existed.

However, she must have been tough, the 'Little Aunt' as she was known in the family. As the youngest of a family of eight she had been brought up in Haddington, a small county town 18 miles from Edinburgh. And this, to my mind, makes it all the more extraordinary that in 1901, at the age of 26, she was despatched to Kansas to nurse one of her elder brother's children who had become sick. But in an era before jet travel and instant communication, it is often surprising to discover just how strong the bonds of family remained. Like so many younger sons of Scottish families, Great-Uncle Patrick had set off to America ten years earlier to become a cowboy. Finding himself in the Sunflower State, he had married Janet Wise, a local girl, and before long they had bought a ranch and started a family. When a son was born and promptly took ill, it was natural for Patrick to call upon the assistance of his youngest unmarried sister. The fact that it would involve a sheltered country girl under taking a sea voyage and overland journey of 5000 miles probably never crossed his mind.

Seven-year-olds have no awareness of the transitory nature of time, but 27 years later I gained some insight into what it must have been like for the Little Aunt when I met Cousin Bill, the child she had travelled all those miles to nurse. By then he was the same age as she had been when I met her, and he was living with his wife, Gyp, a 'southern belle', in Charlotte, North Carolina. Whether or not Cousin Bill genuinely remembered anything at all about the tiny Scots aunty who arrived at his father's ranch by stage-coach in 1901 is doubtful. But he certainly recalled the impact she made on a close-knit Midwest community in the two years before she returned home in 1903. They had all loved her, he told me. Many was the broken heart she left behind among the menfolk when she returned to Scotland. Somehow this was hard to imagine, having known her only in old age.

It was equally difficult to conceive just what it must have been like for a young woman to have to travel on her own across continents by ship and rail and coach and horseback, knowing that urgent messages both to and from home would take months to arrive. Think about it. President William McKinlay had just been shot at the Pan-American Exposition in Buffalo, and Theodore Roosevelt sworn in as America's youngest president to date. Later that year, Guglielmo Marconi signalled the letter 'S' across the Atlantic by wireless telegraph, and it was to be another two years before the first coast-to-coast automobile trip, from San Francisco to New York, took place. You needed courage to cross America in those days.

I bitterly regret having been too young to ask the Little Aunt about her life and her trip to Kansas, and she left no diary that I know of. Back in Scotland, she took up nursing, trained at Edinburgh's Royal Infirmary, then a hospital in Dumfries. This was long before the outbreak of the First World War, but like so many women of that generation, any prospects of marriage were to be blasted by the devastation of the trenches. But even if there had been somebody special, it was her secret. The Little Aunt belonged to a resilient breed of women who preceded universal suffrage. The fact that she had left home to go to work in the first place caused consternation enough among her nearest and dearest. Unmarried daughters from her background were expected to stay at home and look after their parents in their old age. It was the Little Aunt's opinion that her sisters could do that if they wished. She had other ambitions. Defying the social rule books of the middle classes, rebels such as she pioneered the way for the career women of future generations. Before finally retiring to live with her two unmarried sisters in a house on the seafront of North Berwick, the Little Aunt had become matron of Hull City Hospital, alternating with a large fever hospital nearby at Cottingham. A surviving photograph shows her surrounded by her staff, a diminutive, determined figure in starched cap and uniform, dwarfed by those on either side. She died, aged 81, in 1956.

Cousin Bill died in Charlotte in 1984, two years after my first visit to him. He never did cross the Great Pond, as it is called, and the only two of his Scots relatives he ever met were the Little Aunt at the beginning of his life, and myself towards the end. But in his will, he left me an engraved silver salver taken from Scotland to America by Great-Aunt Isobel on her epic American adventure at the turn of the century. It has now come home again and has pride of place on a hall table, a strangely haunting momento of the tiny figure whose fingers I inadvertently shut in a car door when I was seven years old.

Roddy Martine (born 1947) was born of Scottish parents in Kuching, Sarawak. He was formerly the editor of *Scottish Field* magazine, and contributes to a wide range of UK newspapers and periodicals.

Bill Forsyth

❧

Memories of Underdevelopment

In 1955, at the age of nine, I accomplished an astounding feat of social advancement unprecedented in the annals of my family. It happened during a medical examination at primary school, an annual occurrence in those last days of mass urban malnourishment, rickets and TB. During the routine small talk held with the doctor while he prodded and poked and sounded heart and lungs, out of the blue he said, 'How would you like to come on holiday with me to the seaside?' I replied that I would like that very much, and even as I spoke, at the speed of light the fantasy was fixing in my mind: summer, a large house on the fashionable edge of a seaside town, access to a private beach and boat, the doctor's own two children — a biddable boy, slightly older than myself (a big brother!), and the unusually pretty daughter, my own age, and, we discover during many pleasant evening strolls (just we two), of similar dreamy temperament. At leisurely breakfasts, just to earn my keep, I would remember to give the good doctor himself a little of my time, and indulge him in the diverting conversation with me that he obviously relished.

At the end of that school day I rushed home to tell my mother the exciting news, already aware that this first soaring social outing of mine signalled the beginning of the end of the nuclear cohesion of our little family group. I would have to break it to her gently. As my world expanded, however, we wouldn't lose touch, I could assure her of that. I'd write, and visit.

A few weeks later, as I sat in an Education Department basement waiting room with 20 or so other frail or sickly boys, all clutching little fibre suitcases or parcels, the truth had already dawned. The doctor had, in fact, been gently informing me that I was heading for two months of the healthy benefits of a Glasgow Corporation holiday school. I was underweight, a bit skinny (I really did wear belt and braces), in a word I was 'underdeveloped'. Nowadays, you have to be a country to get called that; then it was for kids. What I needed was a spell at Seafield Residential School, a mile up the coast from the Ardrossan oil refinery (its aroma still lingers in the imagination). A grey school bus would magic us there.

It moved me greatly when I recently worked out that this same basement room is now a city trattoria, where I frequently sit in wonderment at my own children as they order their apricot juice and bread with olive oil and pasta primavera and passion fruit sorbets, at twelve years old even expecting the invitation of a splash of watered wine with their Saturday lunch. As they nibble on their pecorino do they sense, seated on hard benches lining the walls, the spectres of all those pasty, puny, sniffling lads of days gone by, including their dad?

We were a busload of strangers, plucked from our separate schools and brought together by the fluke of our various ailments, minor malnourishment, chestiness and post-operative weaknesses. When we reached the coast we were still silent, brooding, each of us dealing alone with what, for all of us, was the first major separation of our lives. Home seemed a galaxy away that first night, all the murmuring talk in the darkened dormitory was of breaking windows and heading for the distant city across the trackless wastes of Ayrshire. My father had often told us of his feelings as a prisoner of war, and now I knew what it was like.

I think that my philosophical sensibilities were fully awoken at Seafield. There were big windows to linger at, to watch the horizons, sea one way and hills the other, and muse on distance and time and aloneness, and how to measure them. Lifelong tasks. I felt similar stirrings in other boys. Sunsets became important for us, we budding existentialists in mandatory short pants. Oddly I can't now remember the names of any of my compatriots. It seems that the Seafield experience was a hermetically sealed event in my life, with no human spillage into the rest of it. Only once, years later, did I think I recognised a fellow inmate driving a Number 20 bus. There was no hope of flagging him down for a reminiscing chat.

The regime at Seafield was a Fifties blend of boarding school and convalescent home. Lessons in the morning were followed by healthy activities in the afternoon. The main one, the only one come to think of it, was walking. We walked everywhere, in regimented lines. To the town to Woolworth's every Thursday with our pocket money, to church on Sundays, to the pictures on Saturdays, and every day to the beach, every single day the crocodile trek to the windswept beach, the tang of crude oil in our nostrils. Discipline was very Fifties, which means almost Victorian. An exposed leg (short trousers, remember) was always the preferred target for Miss Mathieson's expertly flicked ruler in class. Sometimes she would disappear below desk level, down on all fours taking aim. The next thing we'd hear was a yelp. This habit of hers was strangely indulged by us, perhaps because we had no real say in the matter. She was just something that had to be lived with. We tolerated her stings and brushed her off like some natural pest. It revealed to me the admirable stoicism that can be displayed by the put-upon. I was and am proud of my fellows for this display of innate dignity.

The secret of Seafield's success was its food, big cooked breakfasts, and three-course meals twice a day, all mostly stodge. Magically, it made little Michelin men of even the most woeful of waifs in a few short weeks. I saw the distressed expression on my mother's face when she made a visit. She declared that I had been blown up like a balloon. But no worry, within weeks of returning home I was back to my fighting featherweight of old. More to my mother's alarm, once I was home it took me months to stop calling her 'Miss'.

The main building at Seafield was a mock castle, the pride of some Victorian merchant, with a spooky tower, whose creaky staircase we had to climb shortly after our arrival. At the top in a tiny round room was a little lady sitting at a sewing machine. She spent each and every day fixing numbered labels to our clothing. There was a strange fairy-tale feel to her, and we had the impression that she never ever left that tower. I was Number 32. One function of this system was revealed to us when, shortly before the inevitable afternoon walk one day, we were unexpectedly lined up outside the toilet block (an old stable building). We sensed something was up, the edgy atmosphere like a scene from a Colditz movie. Then a teacher emerged from the latrines holding at arm's-length a pair of extravagantly soiled underpants, which had been secreted behind a cistern. She was playing the drama to the hilt (she had seen the same movie). All she had to say was 'Number 41' for a young life to change, perhaps permanently, but certainly for the rest of that day. There would be no beach walk for Number 41. He remained behind to clean his clumsily concealed pants in cold water. That was the sentence. We thought he deserved it. With more savvy he could easily have buried them in the woods or thrown them over a hedge. I wonder now if Number 41 remembers this event, and has been tempted to cleanse its memory by chancing his unlucky number on a lottery ticket.

Wayward bodily functions must have been a symptom of being plucked so cruelly from the family nest. Every morning as we stood to attention by our beds, the duty teacher would run her hand along each exposed bedsheet, checking for night-time wettings. The humiliation of being found out was a trauma to be avoided. I remember spending tortured hours, most of a long night from pitch black to morning glimmer, lying on a damp spot of my own making, successfully drying it with my body heat just before the morning inspection. Teacher's expert fingers passed over and felt nothing.

We were billeted in huts in the grounds, each one named after an aircraft, like Sunderland or Lancaster or Mosquito. In fact, there was a definite wartime air to the whole place, and it crossed my mind that earlier it might have been a haven for evacuee children from our city. This atmosphere was further evoked by an adaptation of a wartime song, re-named the 'Seafield Song', which we were forced to remember with such effect that I still do:

> Bless them all, bless them all,
> the staff down at Seafield we call,
> bless Miss McDonald for all she has done,
> bless dear Miss Woodrow when she's on the run,
> there's Miss Mathieson, Miss Mackay who's so tall,
> they come at our slightest call,
> when we're in a pickle out comes Mrs Nichol,
> and we give our thanks to them all.

The words were written by Mrs Nichol who, it struck me at the time, had awarded herself the best accolade. She got to be comprehensively helpful, while the others were just tall, or scary, or simply there. I noticed things like that.

One memory abides above all other: the nightly washing routine. I had never experienced or even heard of showers before, and even if I had, the showering at Seafield would still be uniquely memorable. Every night after cold milk and bread and jam, we took ourselves upstairs. We stripped and piled under the steaming hot water, to be lathered and scrubbed by the shower ladies, dressed in their rubber aprons and rubber boots and gloves, their hair tied up in scarves, the heady scent of carbolic soap in the air. Then we would line up as the ladies briskly rubbed us dry with big rough towels, while they gossiped amongst themselves, as if we were just so many dolls on a conveyor belt. Finally they would comb our hair through with insecticide. I don't think this ritual had any lasting effect on my adult development (beyond a now largely curbed penchant for automatic car-washes which feature hand finishes), although I confess my ears do buzz a little at the memory of it, and a sniff of certain tarry shampoos does even now provide a frisson. I certainly never told my mother about it, but have stored it away in my creative filing system, for possible use as a Fellini-esque sequence in some film I might make in the future. I am oddly proud that my otherwise drab northern history contains this one nugget of exotic imagery to rival the Italian maestro's own.

Oh, one other memory persists. The memory of a fantasy. The doctor's daughter. I'm still looking for her.

Bill Forsyth (born 1946) has written and directed seven films, including *Gregory's Girl*, *Local Hero*, *Housekeeping* and *Being Human*.

Jimmie Macgregor

'Hurl me to the Central Station, Driver'

The walk from the summit of the Corrieyairick Pass above Fort Augustus across to the Creag Meagaidh nature reserve is a heavy slog on steadily rising moorland. It gets worse, with a steep pull to the 3000 foot plus crest of the horseshoe-shaped cliffs of the Coire Ardair. The fugitive Bonnie Prince Charlie came this way after his defeat at Culloden, and I was following in his footsteps in the making of a television series for BBC Scotland. The huge crescent of the cliff face, with its buttresses and gullies, is broken by a strange V-shaped cleft which acts as a natural funnel, amplifying every whisper of wind. As I came through the fissure, I had the bad luck to encounter the first hail and sleet of the year, and I found myself clinging to the rock as ferocious gusts of wind almost lifted me off my feet. This rocky wind tunnel is known as the window, and by one of those strange trigger mechanisms which suddenly illuminate areas of lost memory, a window opened in my mind and I was taken back to my childhood in Glasgow.

I was pushing six. My brother, Ian, was a little over a year younger. As we turned the corner from Edgefauld Road where we lived, a freak blast of wind came howling up from the waste ground facing Croftbank Street, raising us bodily, and throwing us into the middle of the road. Cars were a rarity in the Springburn area in those days, so that I experienced the clearly remembered sensation of flying, at the cost of no more than a few bruises and some lost skin. Long before I came to know the slopes, corries and ridges of the Scottish hills, I had been familiar with the deep canyons and sandstone cliffs of Glasgow. Strangely, the most powerful evocation of my childhood is the smell of hot tin. Many of the more fascinating of our childhood games and rituals took place in the long, dark winter evenings, and the dim closes, stairwells and dunnies, with their flickering yellow gas-light, provided an environment that was mysterious, exciting, and sometimes frightening. We had cheap torches that flashed white, red and green, and elaborate signalling systems were developed. There were also little four-sided lanterns stamped out of thin tin and lit by a tiny candle. In addition to being skilfully designed to inflict severe lacerations, they heated up very quickly, scorching the hands of all but the most adept signallers. That odour of wax and hot tin is still pungent in my nostrils.

It's fashionable now to sigh over the lost warmth and community of the tenements, but it's noticeable that the sighers are usually of an age to have spent only their childhood in them. An older generation remembers also dirt, poverty and hardship, as well as the continuous struggle to protect their children from those realities. The success of that struggle is what allows people like me to look back through rose-tinted glass. There was, nevertheless, a distinct sense of belonging. Neighbours were always at hand — even when not wanted, it must be said. Doors remained unlocked, and few secrets survived for long. It was always known who was pregnant and whether or not she should be; who was ill; where the old people were and how they were. There was much mutual support, and some bitter feuds, leading occasionally to fisticuffs in the back courts. These encounters were usually ritualised and fairly brief. The women's battles could be much more spectacular, and normally took the form of the 'sterr heid rammy'. Physical encounters were rare, but awe-inspiring. The normal form was the 'sherricking', a modern urbanised form of the more ancient and traditional 'flyting'. This was an exchange of insults publicly conducted at full volume. One combatant in our street became fairly quotable after replying to what she interpreted as a deadly slur, with the words, 'Don't you dare call me a typical!' A lady who became even more famous was Mrs O'Brien. (The false name confers a protection which she certainly does not deserve.) Mrs O'Brien was a real scunner, with a face which my brother, Norman, once described as looking like 'a torn melodeon wi' the tune hingin' oot'. Long-term residence in a wally close and ownership of an aspidistra in a brass pot had given

Mrs O'Brien delusions of adequacy. She was a snob and hated the local children, but not as much as we hated her. Nevertheless, we were enormously impressed when the rumour went round that she was to embark on her holiday by taxi. Taxis were big stuff in Springburn at that time, and this was a real event. On the appointed day, Mrs O'Brien, having pulled a crowd like a Cup Final, appeared at the close mouth, dressed to the nines and sporting a hat which bore about half a stone of ceramic fruit. In the ensuing hush, she strode to the waiting car and, in imperious tones, commanded, 'Hurl me to the Central Station, driver.' Her cover as a sophisticate blown forever, she became a prime target for the kind of persecution which we thought of as fun.

The simplest of our games was the ring and run ploy, which had people jumping up and down answering doorbells. A touch of subtlety could be added to this by sending the most dough-headed of the group to ring the bells on the top landing, while the rest rang the bells at the bottom. With good timing, the escaping ringer would arrive on the ground floor in time to cop a skelp round the ear from an enraged ringee. A variation on the theme was achieved by tying together all the door knobs on one landing, ringing the bells and standing back to enjoy the ensuing tug of war. Simpler, but nastier, was the leaning dustbin. This was carefully balanced against the door. You rang and ran, and the victim opened up to a cascade of smelly garbage all over the lobby. We thought this was really terribly amusing. There was a consensus that the most satisfying games were those that most annoyed, frightened or disgusted people.

Not all of our diversions were irritating. Some were dangerous. The back courts of the tenements were a maze of railings, dykes, wash houses and middens, and much of the time we spent 10, 12, or 15 feet above the ground. There was great competition as to who could make the most impressive leaps between the rooftops. Distance was not the only criterion by which a jump was judged: a row of spiked railings between the two roofs added considerably to the jumper's reputation. All the railings in the back courts were fearsomely spiked and the occasional injury, sometimes serious, was accepted as part of the hazards of tenement life. I have sometimes wondered about those spikes. Did the people who put them there see them perhaps as a deterrent to the disadvantaged hordes intent on breaking into the idyllic life of the tenements?

The girls had an extensive repertoire of skipping and ball games, with their accompanying songs and rhymes, while the boys played wee heidies, or keepie uppie, which consisted of heading a ball against a wall, sometimes hundreds of times. Everyone played street football, and the early training with the tannery ba' (Sixpenny Ball) is said to be the source of the jinky skills which once distinguished our Scottish footballers. Rounders was a popular game, which is why most Scots find the American fanaticism about baseball faintly daft. To us it's just rounders in funny hats. Cricket? No one had ever heard of it. There were also cissy round games like Bee Baw Babbity, which usually involved girls, and even kissing, and were normally played at school under duress.

Much more enjoyable were the confrontations with the kids from the Catholic school. We made faces, uttered what we thought were deadly swearie words, and hurled clods of earth at each other. Little damage was done, and both sides had a great time. No one knew why we fought the Catholics. It was traditional. I didn't really know what a Catholic was, except that the Flynns were nice neighbours with odd pictures on their walls. Those ancient tribal rivalries have almost faded away, though there is a fanatic fringe that tries to keep them alive, but there was a time when an ill-considered answer to the question, 'Are you a pape or a prod?' could get you a rattle on the jaw. It was useless to try 'I'm a Jew', for that simply brought the supplementary question: 'Aye, but are you a papish Jew or a proddy Jew?'

The Scots have accepted people of many races: Polish, Italian, Irish, Lithuanian, Asian, Chinese, African and West Indian, among others. This has been done with the minimum of friction, but perhaps we are still enjoying the remnants of our old prejudices too much to be bothered taking on any new ones. The nearest I've heard to a racist joke comes from the time of the trouble between India and Pakistan, when it was said that we had so many Pakistani lads working on the buses that there was a danger of the Indians bombing Parkhead garage. The orange and the green are just colours now to most sensible people, but in the 1950s an obstreperous wee drunk on the late-night bus from George Square, on being told off by the Nigerian student conductor, retaliated by accusing him of being 'a big orange bastard'.

The life of the tenements ended quite suddenly. In the 1950s and '60s, there was an idealistic, but perhaps not too carefully considered, campaign of slum clearance, as it was called. Great areas of old buildings were razed, and the people decanted into the high-rise housing complexes which have proved to be such a social disaster. The whole project was well-intentioned, but based on modernist architectural theories developed on the Continent and inadequately adapted to Glasgow, with its less comfortable climate and different light. The process of change took place in a startlingly short space of time, and when the old tenement environment disappeared, it scattered long-established communities which never had the chance to regroup. The single-ends, the Jenny a' things, the peeries, the bogies, the girds and cleeks and the coal-fired black grates are now in museums, visited by people still young enough to remember them as part of their everyday lives. The surviving tenements have now been sand-blasted back to their original rich russet, yellow, cream and honey colours. They are refurbished, modernised, much valued, and occupied by quite a different kind of person.

From *Jimmie Macgregor's Scotland*

Jimmie Macgregor MBE **is a household name. As a lover of all things Scottish and with a long career as a folk musician, naturalist, author, lecturer and conservationist, he remains as popular as ever.**

Dr E.M. Armstrong

Learning to Swim by Boat

It was the Germans' fault really, the fact that I had to take the boat to the Dundee baths, but it certainly added to the fun of learning to swim. Before we came back to Fife in 1956, my family had lived in West Hartlepool in the northeast of England. There was a fine indoor pool on the seafront there. Or rather, there had been. For most of my early years, the pool and its whole surrounding area was a sea of rubble as a result of enemy action.

I was not unique, however, in the class I joined at the age of eleven in Castle Hill Primary School in Cupar. None of my colleagues could swim either. Hence the high excitement at the news that the local council were to set up a scheme to take the whole of the top two classes to swimming lessons in Dundee every day of the two-week Easter holidays. East Fife in those days was really quite remote from the rest of Scotland. The train ran south to Edinburgh via a tortuous route through Kirkcaldy or north to Dundee via a change at Leuchars Junction. By road, the two bridges over the Forth at Kincardine and Stirling were over an hour away, as was the Tay crossing at Perth. The fastest way to Dundee baths was by boat over the Tay ferry.

The first day dawned grey and drizzly, as only late March can be in the East Neuk, but spirits were in no way dampened as we assembled outside the Corn Exchange. The two wheezing, single-decker Bluebird buses stood ready, the driver gloriously isolated in his single cabin over the engine at the front. It was a 20-minute drive to Tayport and the start of the next adventure — off the buses, down the ramp to the evocative mixture of smells — diesel oil, seaweed, fish and salt air — that characterized the Dundee ferry. Despite the weather, we made the most of the 15-minute crossing on the upper deck, relishing the odd burst of spray from the grey waters of the rolling Tay as the great city drew closer.

Dundee was a black place in those days, rather down-at-heel. There were stories of great wealth, of jute barons and whaling kings, but the pervading atmosphere to a lad in the 1950s was black. The slip was black. The quay was black. The old wooden training ship we passed on the short walk was black. The baths were black. This was not a leisure complex. But it was not just a swimming pool: it was a baths. It smelt of a now-forgotten mixture of chlorine and carbolic acid. I seem to remember it had steaming caverns, called Turkish baths (not for kids) and cavernous cubicles containing scrubbing brushes, great blocks of brown strong soap, huge coarse towels, and the biggest cast-iron baths we had ever seen. We were there on business, however: to learn to swim.

The pool seemed immense, although I suspect it was only 25 yards long. Everything was white, tiled and clean — except the water, which was opalescent and of a brownish-green tinge. Small pieces of debris gathered in the corners of the deep end, among which, I remember on my first terrifying visit there, were a couple of sweet papers and some cigarette ends. Lessons were organised, regimented, progressive and they worked. The breast-stroke was taught. First the arm movements, then the legs, all practised first on the pool ends, lying astride benches, followed by the first gasping efforts in the freezing pool. Adrenaline is a great antidote to hypothermia. By the Thursday of the second week, the final mystery was revealed: how to co-ordinate the breathing with the rest of the movements so that we breathed out on the glide and in on the recovery. Quite simple really. Then there was a triumphant little line of Fife tadpoles, hesitantly but proudly making their way all round the pool, desperately resisting the temptation to reach out for the rail on the left and trying not to think about either the debris or the depth at the far end.

The highlight of each of the ten days, however, was the return trip on the ferry. There, on the top deck, with the salt wind blowing the scarcely-dried hair, and our teeth chattering with the cold (heated was a relative term when applied to swimming baths), we would open our flasks and unwrap our rolls, fresh that morning from Fisher and Donaldson's in the Crossgate. Mine were always marmalade — heaven!

A colleague, who lives in St Andrews, recently told me that he could get to Perth Royal Infirmary via the Tay Bridge in 25 minutes. Cupar, along with many other Scottish towns, now has a pool of its own. Dundee baths are, I suspect, long demolished to make way for a leisure complex or a water park. It may be progress, but personally I have always been grateful to the Germans for giving me the chance to learn to swim by boat.

Ernest McAlpine (Mac) Armstrong (born 1945) is the Secretary of the British Medical Association.

Hugh Dodd

❦

Our David

Growing up on a farm in East Lothian, not a mile from the sea, offered me a wonderful adventurous playground. I remember the long summer days as my brother, David, and I would roam through the fields toward Tantallon Castle, then scramble down the cliffs to the long sandy beaches of Seacliff to fish at the little harbour or search for shells and crabs amongst the many rock pools, and finally by dusk, wend our way home.

But most of our days were spent playing around the farm, between steading and gardens or on Whitekirk Hill where we went on our great shooting expeditions. Armed with an ancient lever-handled 1920s B.S.A. 177 air rifle, nothing was safe! We were all 'dead-eyed Dicks' with that gun, even my sister, Gay, was a crack shot! All vermin were an open target: mice, rats, crows, rooks, and anything else that moved. However, our sights were always set on something a little more palatable. Our David was particularly partial to wood pigeon, not an easy target, but with time and careful stalking, even that would somehow land on the table — despite my heavy-handed plucking!

Eventually when we were a little older, we were encouraged to join the 'grown-up's shoot' near Nunraw Abbey at the foot of the Lammermuir Hills where we were formally blooded on the August grouse moor. Over the seasons that followed we would also bring back pheasants, partridge, snipe, duck and hare from the lower stubble fields and surrounding woodlands. Much to our delight, we children, too, ate a lot of game.

When we went off to public school, things were very different. David, having preceded me by a year, however, had worked out the ropes. In his wonderfully imaginative way, he had taken certain steps to make our stay there a little more appealing. He had immediately joined the Pet Club, and by the time I arrived he had secured the position of Club Secretary and membership was flourishing. There were hamsters, mice, rabbits, gerbils, and a huge number of guinea pigs (the most popular pet). He had also arranged that the

Club should have access to the first-floor roof of an outhouse above the science laboratory, ostensibly to store spare hutches and bales of bedding straw. But, as it turned out, it was from here that he ran the first of his many 'operations'. When I climbed the ladder to the roof for the first time, I remember hearing a flutter from above and a familiar coo-cooing which stopped me in my tracks. A few steps higher and I soon realised why the Club had proved to be so very popular: a large area of the roof had been sectioned off to create an aviary bursting with beautiful homing pigeons, David's special pets.

That was my first Thursday at school. By the second, I realised the extent of my brother's genius when, with the help of a Spanish cook, I was served Breast of Pigeon in Plum Sauce with chips as a special welcoming treat!

Hugh Dodd (born 1948) is a cartoonist, illustrator, artist and author of several books.

Eddie Bell

High Noon

Saturday afternoon. Airdrie. The late fifties. We huddled together in the darkness, Jim Forbes, Charlie McDade and me. The road stretched out before us, emptied of people. There had been word of this confrontation for weeks; we lads could speak of little else. And now it was going to happen before our nervous young eyes. I remember clutching at Charlie's shirt as the Doctor stepped out. His name was Holliday, and today was the day for killing, not curing. He liked a drink, this man of medicine. He'd already killed a patient by operating on her when he was three sheets to the wind, but retribution was blowing up in his face in the form of the dry, flinty dust of this timber and clapboard New Town, and the local sheriff who was now circling slowly towards him.

To some, childhood is homework, pocket money, cocoa and comic books. To me, the defining moment was the eradication of the evil Clantons by Henry Fonda's Wyatt Earp, and spread-eagling of Victor Mature's Doc Holliday in the baking dust of the OK Corral.

There were three cinemas in Airdrie: the Odeon, the Rialto and that palace of dreams unadventurously baptised The Cinema. Every Saturday morning, we'd gather at the end of my street and run six or seven miles to confront what it is that a man's gotta do. Afterwards, we'd gallop out of the cinema and head for the hills, knowing the Comanches were hot on our heels. If we timed it right — and after years of relentlessly stalking every Western matinee that hit town we had it down to a fine art — we could arrive at the Gartlea Bridge just as the train puffed over it, the smoke billowing out like prairie dust to hide us from the Injuns. As far as I can remember, we were such accomplished cowboys, not a single kid ever lost his scalp to a Comanche tomahawk, although wee Charlie once grazed his head on a stanchion of the bridge and won our everlasting respect for his narrow escape.

Cowboys were big in my young days. My father, who laid kerb-stones for the council, liked a good read and our bookshelves heaved with Dickens, political treaties, and the complete works of Hank Janson. He was a committed Christian Socialist, Dad, and had firm opinions on world politics, particularly Czechoslovakia and Hungary. Politics and cowboys; if we could have materialised for him his own hero, out would have ridden a Communist on Horse-back — the Marxist Kid — the hero on the red stallion.

I was an afterthought in the family, but no less loved for that. I had three siblings: Jean, Jim and Ian — and I arrived 17 years after my elder brother. I had four mothers: Jean (my biological mum), sister Jean, Cathie (Jim's wife) and June (Ian's wife). And I was blessed with three-and-a-half fathers: Jim, Ian, John (Jean's husband) and Dad, when he was in a good mood.

Over-endowed as I was in the parenting department, my early years were cocooned in affection. Mum was the dynamo of the family. She worked in management for the Reo Stakis hotel group, and was responsible for opening Scotland's first dedicated steak-house. Management was not a responsibility she could shuck off like her warm-smelling beige coat when she stepped through the front door at the end of the day. She took upon herself the burdens of the entire street, patching up the quarrels, taking over a stew to an old lady in the house at the end of the road, passing messages between families who no longer spoke to each other.

We bought the first telly in the street and from that day on it was open house. Twenty, thirty guests crammed into our front room, Dad muttering from his chair in the corner, adding his own interpretative sub-text to the news items, Mum bustling back and forward in the kitchen.

She was a great chef, Mum. In my capacity as Chairman of HarperCollins UK I get the opportunity to dine in Michelin-starred restaurants all around the world, but I'd sideswipe cripples and step on old ladies to ensure a table that served up Mum's Special: a large oven-warmed plate of black pudding, eggs, bacon, potato scones and square sausages. (Whenever I hear someone speaking of a 'good square meal', I still think of those sausages.)

After a Saturday morning at the movies, a narrow brush with our feathered pursuers and a hearty meal from Mum, Saturday afternoon was footie practice.

Football. I can only echo Bill Shankley's avowal that football wasn't a matter of life and death — it was far more important than that. My hero was Ian Macmillan who played for Airdrie. I was schizophrenic about my heroes. I can vividly recall a youthful nightmare in which two teams faced each other a minute from end of play, scores level. Taking the penalty was Macmillan himself, and guarding goal was Wyatt Earp. I found my loyalties tested to such an extent I woke up bathed in sweat, a rehearsal in torn loyalties that prepared me slightly for latter-day quandaries between the demands of an insistent best-selling author and the needs of a changing market.

Me, I played left back for my school, Tollbrae. Our team danced its way to the semi-finals until Chaplehall snatched victory from us. A tragic moment. Now if only we'd had Macmillan playing for us, or Wyatt Earp in goal...

Our town was rich in characters.

There was Uncle Alfie, the projectionist, who would come out on stage between the serial and the main feature and entertain us with a ukulele solo, his knee up on a chair, his fingers careering over the strings. Some years ago on a Club outing in Scotland, between the main course and the sweets, an old man of 80 or so came out onto the platform and unwrapped a battered old uke. He was hardly into his first number when a murmur ran through the sober Scottish citizens: My God! It's Uncle Alfie! His old arthritic fingers hadn't lost a single quiver of virtuosity.

Then there was the one-armed newspaper seller who had a sideline in flashing. What an artist! Not only could he fold and hand over a paper and count out the change with one hand but also simultaneously proffer his credentials.

Duncan Donaldson was the local lunatic hard man. Whenever a crime was committed in our area the police would go straight round to his place for a chat, even before the clues had been assembled and studied. He was up in court one day, standing there, glowering at the JP, his eyes burning embers, 137 previous convictions to his credit. The JP shook his head sadly. 'Duncan,' he muttered, 'dear me, don't you think it is time you grew up?' Immediately, Duncan fell on his knees and praised the Lord. When he returned home after a final spell in prison, he built a cross out of railway sleepers in his front garden and spent the rest of his years evangelising. He was a tough cookie, our Duncan, and when he evangelised, you listened. In the autumn of his life, he was probably responsible for more conversions among the locals than his fellow countryman, David Livingstone.

Alfie di Massio was the local ice cream man. His endearing trick was to suddenly pretend he was suffering a heart attack as he handed over your cone — and so dedicated was he, he was prepared to sacrifice the odd scoop of vanilla or rum and raisin in the interests of verisimilitude. He was also something of a ventriloquist; he would throw his agonised yells after you as you fled from his crisis, aiming them so precisely that you'd be convinced he was dying right behind you when he was still in his van.

Wee Jeannie Doig was the local witch. She lived in a tumble-down house with an overgrown garden. No gas, no electricity. We all wondered what she ate, and when one of the lads went missing (he was, in fact, visiting a sick auntie over the border), we were convinced she'd caught him and eaten him raw. Raw! Somehow that made it so much worse. If ever our football went over her fence we'd draw straws for who'd climb over to retrieve it while the others kept guard. Jeannie actually was one of the kindest people in the street. I think, though, that she enjoyed the mythology.

Next door to us lived The Prophet. When I was still tiny, my brother Jim held me feet-up over the fence, dangling me over her garden. One of my socks came off in his hand and I slithered out of his grasp to land on my head. She leaned out of an upper window and shouted out, 'See what you've done! Now he'll never amount to anything!'

Amounting to something. Beyond playing for Scotland, or perhaps cleaning up the local cattle rustlers, none of us harboured any dreams of escaping from Airdrie and seeing our names up in lights. There was nothing to escape from. We were happy there. My childhood was certainly not utopian. Dad could get mean and grumpy and had a fierce back-hand, and at school we all had to learn to fight our corners, but the odd, deserved swipe didn't make me the abused child it's suddenly so fashionable for celebrities to lay claim to.

Looking back now, all the lessons were in place in that first decade. Dad and Hank Janson taught me the art of confrontation without anger (to this day I never lose my temper), Mum taught me management by negotiation, and Chaplehall taught me how to accept defeat without thinking it was the end of the world. Perhaps something did happen to me when my head struck a rock in the next door garden, but when I thought about it later, there were no hard feelings towards Jim. Why should there be? Wyatt Earp would get him. He always did. It was only a matter of time.

Eddie Bell (born 1949) is the Executive Chairman and Publisher of HarperCollins UK.

David Rintoul

Beam-walking

When I was seven we moved house. It was a fine, formal, granite building in the West End of Aberdeen with high ceilings and dark wood and built mainly on two floors. I say mainly because on the second floor a door opened onto a steep staircase which led to a landing and an L-shaped room. This we divided into two: a playroom and, beyond, my bedroom. Around all this, an attic. Access by a small door in the landing. Inside the attic, boards which supported the usual pile of suitcases and junk. One light bulb illuminated the boarded part and dimly lit the unboarded part which started round the corner. So you have the geography.

Dire warnings were given about the unboarded part. You could walk from beam to beam but in between was plaster. One slip and you would hurtle amid plasterwork and light fittings into a bedroom below. Death — or thoroughly justified parental wrath. Great sport, therefore, this beam-walking.

Once, I was alone in the attic and beam-walked further than I ever had before — round the second corner and into almost complete darkness. There in front of me was a battered brown suitcase. I pulled it to the edge of the light and opened it.

Inside, a skeleton.

Seven-year-old child examines skeleton in the dim light. Heart thumping — his — the skeleton's long gone. In fact it's just over half a skeleton. One leg, one arm; the foot and hand each made entire by rough brown twine. All those tarsals and carpals and metatarsals. Rough twine through the vertebrae made a creaking, wiggly spinal column. Individual ribs rattled around the dusty check-patterned bottom of the suitcase. And terrible best of all was the skull. The cranium had been neatly cut round and the top held in place by a brass hook and eye on either side. Lift it up — the skull doffs its top in a gesture of macabre politesse and inside all the shapes like coral underwater. The mandible was held in place with smart brass springs. Open wide. Teeth gone, I'm afraid. Snaps shut like a mousetrap. Seven-year-old child shuts case. The skeleton became, as you can imagine, a bit of a thing.

I was going to say that I had an over-active imagination as a child. Who says? What uniforms do the imagination police wear? Anyway, at half past two at night in my bedroom eyrie with the wind gusting off the North Sea and the rain in rattling, uneven spatters on the window, the skeleton did often come to mind along with all sorts of other terrible imaginings and the only way to get rid of these terrible imaginings was to confront them face-skull face-on. Pyjamaed and cold of foot I'd go across the landing, under the dark, wind-rattled skylight, into the attic, beam-walk to the edge of the light, open the case, meet the eyeless gaze, close the case and best/worst of all beam-walk and rush but not rush back to bed and, the quilt tightly over my head, sleep.

Two years later, I knocked on the door of my father's study. Dad, there's a skeleton in the attic. A what? Skeleton. Unbelieving inter-rogation. Case produced and opened on the study floor. Good heavens I'd forgotten all about that. I had that when I was a medical student. And then, in a kindly and considerate attempt at de-mysti-fication, the naming of these bones which I knew so intimately. In fact I had found out most of their names already. The half pelvic bone held up. Female. You see how it swings out. Childbirth. And I think she died rather old. Funny, and I may be wrong, but I think she might have been black. A breadth in the nasal area. Nine-year-old child de-mystified.

Except. Except that thereafter when the wind howled and the window rattled and I went to have a look at my skeleton, it wasn't just bones I was looking at. I was looking at what had been a very old, black granny in a rocking chair. And she was looking back at me.

David Rintoul (born 1948) is a stage and television actor who has worked with both the Royal Shakespeare Company and the National Theatre. His leading roles on television include Mr Darcy in the BBC's 1980 version of *Pride and Prejudice* and STV's *Dr Finlay*.

Deedee Cuddihy

Knickers

My brother and I had been to at least ten different schools in our young lives so when, after the death of our parents, we were told by the uncle who had become our legal guardian that we were to be sent to a boarding school called Kilquhanity, we were not much bothered. Indeed, the fact that it was in Scotland, 3000 miles away from our home in New York, made the prospect quite exciting. Someone in my last school had done a project on Scotland so I knew that the people there wore kilts and ate things called scones. As it turned out, the founder and headmaster of the school, John Aitkenhead, wore a kilt and, in addition, was a dedicated Scottish Nationalist.

Kilquhanity, I should explain, was no ordinary educational establishment. It was what was known as 'progressive' and was based on the more famous — or infamous — Summerhill school in England, also founded by a Scot, A.S. Neill. Basically, a progressive school was one where you didn't have to go to lessons if you didn't want to, called the teachers by their first names, and had a say in the running of the place at a weekly council meeting (although 'John A.', as the head was known, kept the pupils' more outrageous suggestions in check with what he chose to call 'over-ruling proposals'). Kilquhanity was small, with an average roll of fewer than 50 pupils, so the addition of two teenagers from what was, in the early 1960s, something of an alien culture, could have had quite an impact.

Because of its child-centred ethos, the school attracted a largish number of what could be termed 'emotionally fragile' kids (John A., however, believed that it was often the parents who were emotionally fragile) and although my brother and I, aged 16 and 14 respectively, were really quite normal, our behaviour was probably monitored — but not in any strict sense — in those first weeks for signs of major personality defects. Of the two of us, my brother may have seemed the most well-balanced. He was very outgoing and gregarious while I appeared rather quiet and withdrawn — or so I was later told. My insistence on wearing sun glasses — even at night — and my hair hanging down across one eye, probably didn't help. The fact is, I took longer than my elder sibling to assess new acquaintances and decide if I wanted to put out the welcome mat.

Anyway, the school cook, who was somewhat less child-centred in her attitudes than the rest of the staff, had come to the conclusion that I was a queer fish who needed to be watched. A whiz with birthday cakes, fruit crumbles and jam tarts but with no talent at all for savoury dishes (her boiled egg curry in particular was unbelievably awful), Mrs Moore — no one called her by her first name, not even, I suspect, her husband — was also in charge of the school laundry and when she discovered that I owned 14 identical pairs of white cotton-knit underpants, she immediately reported the matter to her colleagues.

I still can't remember why I had so many. While agreeing that 14 pairs seemed somewhat extravagant, in the days when three were the norm, they didn't feel that it pointed to anything more sinister than, perhaps, a mild anxiety about personal hygiene.

But Mrs M. was not to be put off. She kept me in her sights and, a short time later, caught me engaged in an activity which, she believed, provided conclusive evidence that I was a profoundly disturbed individual. Staff learned that, while snooping around in the girls' dormitory one morning, the cook had secretly observed me 'cutting up a pair of trousers, then sewing them back together again'. Well, this did indeed sound bad. Was the new girl a potential candidate for the local loony bin? A psycho-in-waiting who might, at some point in the future, attack herself or others with the school pinking shears?

In fact, the truth was much less alarming. My brother had given me a pair of jeans he had grown too tall for and I had cut several inches off the legs, then turned the bottoms up to make a hem.

Mrs Moore and I never did become friends, but a married couple, teachers at the school, took on the role of my surrogate parents and we remain close to this day.

Kilquhanity closed its doors in June 1997, but I will be forever grateful to John A. and Morag, his wife, for providing me and my brother with three years of stability in what had previously been a life of considerable emotional turmoil.

Deedee Cuddihy (born 1948) never returned to the United States to live. She is married to a Scot and has two children. She is a writer and freelance journalist.

Donald Meek

❦

Hurricane Betsy

The harvest was almost secure. The fields of our croft were studded with little stacks of hay, the result of weeks of labour — cutting, turning, drying and gathering the crop. Very soon the grey Ferguson tractor, with its yellow buckrake, would carry these small piles into the stackyard, where they would be taken apart with effort, and built into the larger stacks which would provide food for the animals into the spring of the following year. One more piece of sustained labour, one more week of perspiration, and the winter's supply would be safe. The harvest was already running late.

On that Saturday afternoon, back in September 1961, the autumn suddenly lost its golden colour. As I pressed my nose against the glass window of the main door, I could scarcely believe what I saw. The stacks which were sitting so contentedly in the fields less than 12 hours previously were now leaping into the air, and spiralling upwards, like uncontrollable reels of cotton which had suddenly decided to burst apart and defy the forces of gravity. As they disintegrated in the air, bunches of hay began to entangle themselves on the wire fences, and soon the fences were cracking under the strain. Rows of stobs and posts, once standing like soldiers on parade, bent over and snapped as the hay covered the wire, providing yet another barrier for the wind. Dislodging themselves once more, strands and tufts of hay took off across the machair, leaving a wispy trail of dispersed shreds.

The wind battered the house. It had stood there since 1891, and it would not be moved now. Yet Hurricane Betsy put on her best show. She excelled the expectations of the weather forecasters, whose grim litany — 'Malin, Hebrides, Minches. Storm force 10, gusting severe storm force 12, now imminent' — had crackled across the radio as a gale warning early that morning. Sweeping her way in from the Atlantic, Betsy was in no mood for compromise. Formerly a fully-fledged hurricane swinging over from Florida, and now in the last stages of her destructive life, she was determined to wreak as much havoc as possible before she spent herself in an assault on the mountains of the Scottish mainland. She made the waves explode as she sped across the ocean. By evening she had passed over. The rain which came in her wake terminated the weak efforts of the wisps of hay which now lay dying on the sodden land.

Sunday dawned calm and brilliant. Bald humps of brown and lifeless hay contrasted with green grass. The surrounding islands were clothed in their morning glory — Gunna like a green stone crocodile, Coll with its white mouth of western sand, Mull with its cool volcanic peaks, standing boldly in the south-east. Taking my usual walk along the shore, hoping to find a fascinating piece of driftwood or a letter in that ever-elusive bottle, I saw another message, strewn along the glittering shells. Hay was everywhere. Driven by Betsy's relentless pressure, some of it had found shelter below the sand-dunes, and had made friends with the seawrack. Land and sea had become one as the whirlwind battered all into submission.

The sea groaned on the shore, but on the land, the stillness was audible. It was difficult to breathe without disturbing the peace. As a family we discussed the intensity of the storm of the previous day, and went to church as usual. 'God is our refuge, and our strength', said the preacher (my father) as he began the first prayer. Gaelic psalmody was heavy on the lips of the congregation, and the crofters supplemented their morning devotions by discussing the extent of their losses. Hay on the shoreline was an unusual experience, even by the standards of the wind-swept island of Tiree.

What would we do for the winter? Where was the hay crop now? Where was the thanksgiving of harvest? There was a frightened tone to the Gaelic conversation. As a family, we saw it at its worst. The hay would have to be gathered again, every precious wisp. If not, the bills for winter feed would be greater than the income from the croft...

Worst of all, we faced the prospect of breaking the Sabbath. Our guests, coming from the big city of Glasgow for their autumn holiday, had been delayed. The aircraft was grounded because of the Saturday storm. Now they were arriving on Sunday. Warily we met them from the aircraft, and trundled homewards in our blue van. Visitors, at a time like this...

But they had not come to rest, if there was work to be done. That genial couple who had spent their lives facing their own challenges in the city were made of sterner stuff. Day by day, for most of their 'holiday', they patiently combed the wisps of hay off the fences, left them to dry, put them back into piles, and waited for 'little grey Fergie' to carry the heaps for stacking by my father's strong hand. They gathered every shred they could find.

Soon there were untidy stacks on the fields, but this time they did not go into the stackyard. They were carried straight into the barn, and stored in safety. Returning from school, I found myself pressed into service, driving the Ferguson with load after load, until the darkness descended, and my eyes could not see the road ahead.

A fortnight later, the barn was full, although the stackyard was empty. It would be a poor winter, that was certain, but it would be a rich winter, too. Hurricane Betsy had done her worst, but the stackyard of experience was well filled.

Donald E. Meek (born 1949) has been Professor of Celtic at the University of Aberdeen since 1993. A native of Tiree, he was raised on his father's croft in Caolas. Educated locally until he was 16, he went to Oban High School, and then to the Universities of Glasgow and Cambridge.

Barbara Dickson

❀

John, Paul, George, Ringo... and Barbara

At the beginning of 1963 I was in my fourth year at school at Woodmill Junior High in Brucefield, Dunfermline. It was at the start of the first huge wave of Beatlemania and the Fab Four had already had a minor hit with 'Love Me Do', and 'Please, Please Me' was beginning to make them into the phenomenon they were to become. I heard through the grapevine that they were to play a concert in Kirkcaldy at the Carlton Cinema.

I was obsessed with the notion that if I didn't go immediately to the Carlton Cinema for tickets there would be none left, so I set off on my bike to cycle the 15 miles to Kirkcaldy. I am a Libran, and nobody puts me off when I've the bee in my bonnet. I got there in a state of physical collapse and nervous breakdown, having worked myself into a frenzy of hope and doubt on the way, only to be told that ticket applications had to be made by post! I cycled back to Dunfermline even quicker to mail off my money and in due course the tickets arrived. It's interesting to note that the Carlton Cinema wasn't a huge venue, so the Beatles' popularity was still being viewed cautiously in Fife!

The concert was glorious. Music? What music? I just screamed and drooled like the rest of the entire audience and left well satisfied. And I didn't let the side down by wetting the seat: I'm a Scot. My friends who came along were privileged in that one had a Dad with a car. There was no sound of rubber on tarmac that night as four girls, dressed to kill, circa 1963, pedalled along the Aberdour road. We rode home in style, exhausted, post John, Paul, George and Ringo. Bliss!

Barbara Dickson (born 1947) is a singer and actress.

Harriet Bowes-Lyon

Tartan Blood

I think it would be dishonest to say I had a wholly Scottish childhood as, although a Scot by blood, I was actually brought up in England. However, I was taught from an early age by my mother that nothing English was quite right. The church services were wrong and their windows too ornate. None of the fields were the right shape or size, and the people (with a few exceptions) were not nearly as friendly, good-humoured or obliging as the Scots.

With this early indoctrination, it never occurred to me that I would live anywhere other than in Scotland or marry anyone else but a hairy-kneed Scotsman! In fact, so tartan-blooded was I that the Scottish Nationalists, had they known, might well have adopted me as their mascot and *Braveheart* surely pales into insignificance!

Luckily, to quench my thirst for all things Scottish, we spent most of our summer holidays in Scotland and occasionally came north at Christmas or Easter, too. The excitement at crossing the Tay Bridge on the night sleeper before we pulled into Dundee station or the joy of alighting on the platform at Newtown St Boswells, when going to stay at my mother's childhood home, was indescribable. In later years, after Beeching had closed so many of the railways, we used to drive North. Coming past the Kielder Reservoir in Northumberland and knowing that the Scottish border was not too far away was a sensation of pure joy I shall never forget. The journey south again, however, was a melancholy affair.

It will be no surprise to learn that my favourite garment was my kilt. Because I was a girl, for some reason I was not allowed to have a tartan one like my younger brothers, but had to content myself with the Shepherd's Plaid. I was, nevertheless, extremely proud of it and would have worn it all day and night given the chance. Even south of the border we often put on our kilts. My brothers wore theirs to children's parties and on high days and holidays such as Christmas and Easter. This made me a little envious as on occasions such as these I had to wear a party dress. What I should have given to be a boy!

One incident which I shall never forget was when we were staying in the Borders with my uncle and had been invited to the Edinburgh Military Tattoo. It was the first time my brothers and I had ever been allowed to go to the Tattoo and as guests of the Admiral taking the salute that night, we were to sit in the Royal Box and travel to Edinburgh with a police escort. Naturally, we had to be smartly turned out and so my brothers were to be dressed in their kilts and I in the proverbial party dress.

Despite this, nothing was going to extinguish the excitement I felt until, that is, I found my youngest brother sitting firmly on the floor in his bedroom, surrounded by my mother and nanny in some consternation. He was refusing point blank to wear his kilt. I could not believe it possible that he was rejecting this revered garment. I was immediately convinced he must be a changeling. How could anyone related to me NOT like his kilt? (I suspect in retrospect some horrid little boy or girl down south had accused him of wearing a skirt.) So adamant was he, and since there was a danger we might be late if this farce continued much longer, my mother had to give in and he went to the Tattoo in a pair of shorts. I was incredulous and mortified at my brother's treachery, especially when I myself was longing to be in full Highland dress. As far as I was concerned the evening was ruined — or nearly!

Harriet Bowes-Lyon (born 1952) is the President of the Scottish Council of Save the Children.

Ruth Wishart

❧

The Team Players

My brother was not as other boys. Or rather not as my father expected boys to be. He displayed an inexplicable lack of curiosity about the Saturday soccer results, showed very little interest in accompanying his Dad in his lifetime pursuit of a single figure handicap at the gowf, and, when he did take to sport, wound up as the cox in a rowing crew. It wasn't the kind of activity much recorded in the sporting annals of a family wedded to golf, tennis, footie and the long distance worship of the Scottish soccer team.

Thus it was that the girl child was wheeled in as a surrogate son; not the same as the real thing of course, but the only available sub on the bench. When I was deemed tall enough I was taken to Hampden. Tall enough, that is, to stand in front of the seats in the front row and peer over the wooden partition at the wondrous happenings on the field. I was six and I was hooked.

There were other rewards. Sweeties passed surreptitiously into the bedroom if I recited the Scotland team by name in the correct formation. My father took that kind of homework very seriously indeed. He was on the golf course the day that Scotland lost 9-3 to the Auld Enemy and three-putted every hole thereafter. It was rumoured that he was instrumental in setting up a fund to hasten Frank Haffey, the luckless goalie, in his emigration to Australia. But I think not. Having resigned himself to the thought that I was the nearest thing to a sporty heir on offer, he set to the rest of my further education with a will.

The postage-stamp back green was shaved into submission not to please the horticultural sensitivities of my mother, but so that her best bone-handled dinner knives could be pressed into service at the four clothes poles as golf holes. Endlessly we putted round that square. Endlessly the operation failed to make any significant dent in either of our scores.

The professional at his club was also pressed into service. After school there would be an hour's tuition devoted to chipping into a bucket with a sand wedge. Given the amount of my youth thus misspent, it is dispiriting to report that my short game never became anything resembling a strength. However, I never did acquire that paralysing fear of bunkers which afflicts friends who spent more time with a French primer than a nine iron.

Tennis was a must. Dad had been on the local team so it mattered that his daughter could at least make a decent fist of a bounce game. Table tennis, too, the topspin serve perfected on a table fashioned from a bit of hardboard balanced precariously on a card table outside the back door. Mother preferred this sporting duo in al fresco mode. Ever since that nasty little accident when grandfather's prized heirloom — an elaborately carved barometer — had fallen victim to one of my father's more exuberant attempts to chip the goalie when we were playing one-a-side in the hall. Given the height of the 8-year-old goalie, it was a bit of a cheek. At any rate that was a red card job, and we were advised that future soccer fixtures would not be a feature of the indoor sporting calendar.

On Saturdays, I had a special job. That was the night I was dispatched to the newsagent for the 'pink' edition of the Glasgow *Evening Times* with all that day's scores. Impatient to check his coupon, he'd tell me off for reading it from cover to cover as I dawdled back home.

But he never stayed mad for long. Blessed with a sense of humour and a streak of mischief, he couldn't let the pauses between laughter last too long. His favourite pastime — outside of watching Scotland annihilate England 1-0 — was to fill the house with friends, give them hospitality, and cajole them into daft games. This made it a very special childhood, one characterised by the priceless gift of security, and the unquestioning love of two committed parents.

He died when I was fourteen — a jarring punctuation point in all our lives. The day of his death an aunt came to take me shopping, to take me out of the house where my distraught mother tried to come to terms with the rawness of her new grief. I remember seeing people laughing in the street, and hearing banter exchanged in the dairy. And wondering how they could possibly behave so crassly when the sun had just gone in; the world had stopped turning.

Any girl misses her father when he's absent from the next major changes of gear in her life. Misses his presence at her 21st birthday, her marriage, the occasion of her new jobs. But set against the disappointment was 14 years of solid support, love, comfort, laughter. All the things which give children the confidence to grow and explore their potential. A truly bounteous legacy.

I still miss him badly in middle age. But I can still recite the Scotland team. In the right formation.

Ruth Wishart is a journalist and broadcaster. Her husband, Rod, is a cartoonist. Her dog, Dougal, does pretty much what he likes.

Brian Souter

Shopping is Stressful

In common with other male members of the species, I hate shopping and small wonder when I tell you my story.

My mother insisted on sending me to the shops twice a week. This involved a half-mile run along the terrace, through the dump, down the hill, across the road past the swings and round the corner to the

Co-op stores. It was then necessary to secure two loaves, order a bag of coal and pay for the newspapers. In addition to administering the cash, our Co-op dividend number — 3234 — had to be recited at each counter and receipts collected.

As a nine-year-old I coped well with these intellectual challenges and responsibilities but why did Mum insist on my using a large yellow circular plastic basket into which the bread did not fit? This yellow basket got ridicule from my pals and physical threats from the Rannoch Road gang who hung out at the swings.

One day on my return trip, the inevitable happened. I was trapped by a group of ten boys, taunted about my yellow basket and challenged to a fight by a new arrival to the gang called Johnny whose initiation task was to 'take me'. Being small and slow, I had no choice but to fight. The basket and the bread were scattered as I grappled with the bigger boy until, eventually, I pinned him down and extracted a submission.

Shopping in future was less stressful and I walked to the shops instead of running. But old habits die hard. I still use a plastic carrier bag to transport my business files and personal belongings. People say this has become one of my trademarks!

Brian Souter (born 1954) is the executive Chairman of Stagecoach Holdings plc.

Kathy Galloway

❀

Edinburgh Vignette

You're doing your Brownie Housewife badge.
Tidy these drawers, she said,
the public-spirited Morningside lady.
They're my daughter's.

*I don't expect you've ever seen
so many nice things*, she said,
to the ten-year-old from the housing scheme.

Oh yes, you said,
burning with indignation.
I have as many.

❀

Heredity

When I was a child,
my mother sang songs.
Old songs,
about goodwives and fishwives and stockings of silk:
I know where I'm going, and I know who's going with me...
songs from the radio,
take my hand, I'm a stranger in Paradise...
and
que sera sera, whatever will be will be...
songs from the shows,
*tonight, tonight, won't be just any night,
tonight there will be no morning star...*
sacred songs,
I know that my Redeemer liveth...
My mother was always singing.

When I was a child,
my grandmother told stories,
about long-ago weddings
we drove round the loch in a pony and trap, and the driver
had
white satin ribbons on his whip
and brothers who went off to long-ago wars
that was your great-uncle Jack, he died in
the Boer War...
and never-met cousins in far-away places
there's Patsy in Melbourne and Harry in Canada...
and people she'd talked to in stations and tearooms
I met this awful nice young man while I was
waiting for the bus, he gave me his address
and asked me if I'd write to him...
My grandmother was always telling stories.

When I was a child,
my father was always going to meetings,
I'll be late tonight, Janet
getting people to do things,
believing that they could,
riding off on an old bike round the place.
Everybody knew him,
hi, Mr Orr...
implacable with MPs
that communist minister...
about the Bomb and South Africa.
When he had time, he followed the Hearts,
but my father was always going to meetings.

I see now that football
has been my main dissent from heredity!

Child's Heaven

I remember, I remember
the first time I visited Helensburgh Public Library
(staying with my gran);
the wood panelling,
the musty smell,
the sun falling along the floor
in long shafts of shimmering dust,
and all those books!

My insides dissolved
and flooded with ecstasy.
I thought I had arrived in heaven.

**Kathy Galloway (born 1952) is a theologian, poet and activist.
She grew up in Edinburgh, but now lives in Glasgow
with her three teenage children.**

Alex Salmond MP

For Whom the Bells Toll

Throughout my otherwise happy and carefree childhood I laboured under one crushing disadvantage. My birthday is on Hogmanay. This may seem a small matter to those who have never experienced the indignity of being birthday challenged. However, on behalf of my fellow sufferers it is now time to speak out. It is time to share our pain.

Things got off to a pretty mixed start. I was born at home in Linlithgow and within the sound of St Michael's bells. This makes me a bona fide 'black bitch' — a title which not only now confirms the opinion of my political opponents but was not then the sort of moniker you go around boasting about in the playground of Lithca Primary. On the other hand, things might have been even more awkward if I hadn't made it into the world a day or so early. Faither would not have been best pleased if he'd had to miss the Ne'erday match at Tynecastle in the golden era of Conn, Bauld and Wardhaugh. As it was he was able to welcome his first-born son into the world and then go off to the match with a clear conscience if not a clear head.

Being born anywhere near Christmas is not a childhood asset when it comes to birthday celebrations. Admittedly things could have been worse. Christmas Day itself would have been an even bigger problem. A Christmas Day baby effectively loses its birthday altogether after the initial novelty and the attention of the nurses drooling over it. Having a birthday just after Christmas is almost as bad. I always had to live with the fear that friends and relatives were about to run out of dosh before my big day.

One compensation was that people by and large did not forget my birthday. Hogmanay is a pretty easy date to remember. However, as all Yuletide babies will confirm, aunts and uncles tend to combine Christmas and birthday presents in the same parcel. A dear lady — long gone now — used to give me without fail a pair of cotton socks each and every birthday. Nowadays this would be a pretty acceptable present. As a boy I was less than thrilled, not least because I harboured a totally unworthy suspicion that she was recycling the in-laws' Christmas present to her husband.

I worry about the poor unfortunates who are condemned to an end-of-year anniversary. Some people have never recovered from these early birthday setbacks. Perhaps some of the flaws in the character of Hogmanay baby Bonnie Prince Charlie were sourced in effectively missing out on his childhood birthdays. In addition, Hogmanay 1745 (and later birthdays) can't have been a bundle of laughs for the Young Pretender, although he did rather better than many of his followers, who didn't have any more birthdays to celebrate...

For those of us who have been able to put these childhood disappointments behind us and have made it into adulthood as complete human beings, an end-of-year anniversary can swing to your advantage. It gives you a good conversation piece if you appear on Hogmanay TV programmes. And it becomes pretty satisfying to delude yourself that an entire nation is joining in your birthday celebrations, and what's more you have a double excuse for having one — or several — over the eight before and after the Bells.

But wouldn't life be much fairer if, like racehorses, we all were given the same birthday, preferably in the middle of summer. Alternatively, like the Queen, we could all have two anniversaries — one real one and one for official purposes.

…But life is not fair, and until we build that better world, Hogmanay babies will have to make it just the best way we can. In the meantime you, too, can help by making that special effort to remember us during the season of goodwill.

Alex Salmond (born 1954) is the Member of Parliament for Banff and Buchan and is Leader of the Scottish National Party. This first appeared as an article in the *Herald*, 1st January 1997.

Janice Galloway

Objective Truth and the Grinding Machine
or
Don't Let the Bastards etc. etc.

When I was very wee I didn't read at all. I listened. My mother sang Elvis and Peggy Lee songs, the odd Rolling Stones hit as they appeared. These gave me a notion of how relationships between the sexes were conducted (there were no men in our house), the meaning of LURV (i.e. sexual attraction and not LOVE which was something in English war-time films that involved crying); a sprinkling of Americanisms (to help conceal/sophisticate the accent I had been born into and which my mother assured me was ignorant and common) and a basic grounding in ATTITUDE (known locally as LIP). This last, was the most one. In fact, the only useful one. The words to BLUE SUEDE SHOES are carved on my heart.

I was reading by the time I went to primary school. I know because I got a row for it. Reading before educationally permissible was pronounced SERIOUSLY DETRIMENTAL TO HER IN CLASS. This was true because I had to do it again their way, with JANET and JOHN and The DOG with the RED BALL. Books were read round class i.e. too slow, and you got the belt if you got carried away and keeked at the next page before you were allowed to. Kidding on you weren't interested became an intrinsic part of education. This did not trouble me. I was a biddable child. Most are.

At home, I read OOR WULLIE and THE BROONS. I read the BEANO and liked DENNIS THE MENACE but thought BERYL unlikely. The BUNTY was best because it had GIRLS in it. I loved Wee Slavey (the maid with the heart of gold) and the Four Marys (who went to boarding school). Only the former seemed a role model, however. I also read Enid Blyton Fairy Tales (but not the FAMOUS FIVE dear god no) and Folk Tales of Many Lands, the whole set in the local library. I read the Folk Tales over and over then began fingering the mythology and World Religion books on the adult shelves whereupon the librarian (or Defender of books from the inquiry of Grubby People and Children) smacked my hands and told me I wasn't allowed *those ones*: I would neither like nor understand them and was only SHOWING OFF. This was another timely lesson in the value of hiding natural enthusiasm because it sometimes annoyed people in authority who preferred OBEDIENCE TO RULES as more suitable. I didn't stop looking: I stole it. I ran errands to the same library for my nineteen-years-older sister who read six books a week and hit me (literally) if I brought back books by women authors. *Women canny write*, she'd say: *Women canny write*. Other hitting offences included being sent a subscription to *Reader's Digest* by an uncle who didn't know any better, asking to watch *A Midsummer Night's Dream* on the telly and keeping a diary. Enjoying words was an occupation fraught with pain, full of traps, bombs and codes. Worse, it was addictive. Earlier than I learned to do the same thing with sex, I learned to look as though I wasn't doing it at all and became devious as hell.

Thrillers, adventures and war stories caused no ructions. They were the things my sister liked. My mother read too, mostly biographies of film stars — to learn how they'd escaped, I suppose. Some of the film stars she read about were women but they hadn't written the books themselves so that was ok. She also read the odd novel from a stack on top of the cupboard shelf which I could not reach. They had pictures of women with their frocks falling off on the covers and the name Angelique featured on the spines. I already knew enough to know she was not the author. My father had apparently been a reader but he'd been dead for ages and not around much before that either. His books — from a club — were stacked at the bottom of a cupboard. The only one that looked as if it might have jokes was a big black tome with gold letters on the side: *The Complete Plays of Bernard Shaw*. I stole it too. At ten, I accidentally wrote a novel in blue biro and pencil in which the lead character, a BOY my own age who lived in a colonised nation, died horribly after saving his family and village from invading Normans, whereupon the aforementioned family realised, too late, what bastards they had been to him all along. My mother found it but didn't tell my sister. She lit the fire with it.

Secondary school proved mother and sister uncannily perceptive. *Women couldny write*. There were none, not one, not even safely dead ones like Jane Austen or the Brontes, as a class text. Women who appeared in the books by men were seldom the central characters, or if they were, were usually SYMBOLIC. This helped reinforce the notion that women were not interesting in themselves and that ART did not concern itself with them. It took a bit longer to compute that *them* was *us*. *Me*. From there it was only a short step to work out that the more something was about or by women, the less likely it was to be ART at all. This troubled me a fair amount. It meant ART was on my sister's side. To hell with that then. Books would let you down. I fell out of love with BOOKS and intensified being in love with MUSIC because nobody had told me (not yet anyway) that *women canny compose*. The Head of Music became a beacon and my sister couldn't say boo because he was a TEACHER. He taught me MOZART was pronounced MOTZART and not as spelled on the biscuit tin at home. He taught me lots of things. Through third to sixth year, I sang and played Purcell and Byrd, Britten, Warlock and Gesualdo (my sister's aversion therapy meant I could have nothing to do with something called ROMANTIC music, even if it was by men) and read and sang FOLK SONGS. I had always sung pop songs but these ones were old and some were written as though women might be singing them. There were songs about being pregnant, about men, working, raising children. This was not ART of course, but it was exciting. Dangerous even. My mind was made up. I would go to Uni and study MUSIC and be a CREDIT TO MYSELF. Also it would be one in the eye to Head of Girls who said I was *not university material*. The day I was leaving, I turned up at school in trousers and got sent home. This did not trouble me. I was taking the music and getting out. I visited Hillhead, peering out the filthy windows of a 59 bus, salivating. I was on the threshold of being able to let my enthusiasm out to play without apology or concealment. I would revel in Great Works of Music and ponder the meaning of Profound Literary Texts. I couldn't wait.

I should have. Of my English syllabus, less than two of the authors on the set list were female, and only one was Scots. My music list seemed not to know women — or Scotland — existed at all. There were no folk songs. In my third year, I cried a lot and they let me have a year out. I was, I realised with embarrassment, suffering from a broken heart. I went back and finished only because my advisor (whom I saw three times in my whole Uni career) said, *Girls often give up, it's nothing to be ashamed of.* Books were bastards. I could no longer listen to music. There was only one thing for it.

Teaching. On teaching practice, I turned up at school in trousers and was sent home. Finally posted, the store-room was familiar too. On the suggested reading list for senior pupils, there were thirteen women on a list of over sixty authors. Of those, ten, including Jane Austen, the Brontës and Jessie Kesson, were classified under the heading LOVE AND ROMANCE; Muriel Spark's *Prime of Miss Jean Brodie* was a SCHOOL STORY. After the crying stopped, I started laughing and the laughing started something on a slow simmer at the back of my brain. After ten years and lots of reading I tracked down by myself, that simmer melted down all the bloody nonsense I'd been led to believe about AUTHORSHIP, WOMEN, SCOTLAND, CLASS and ART. And at last, like E.M. Forster, I could CONNECT. I could connect reading lists with straitjackets, the university with Saltcoats Library, and my sister with Hitler.

It was like finding the nose on my face.

It was better because, for the first time since I learned how to pronounce MOZART, it suggested I had the right to know things too. I felt the dangerous rush of FREEDOM in place of the RULES and I started to remember things. I remembered things I had known from a long time ago. I remembered Elvis. And I knew three things. I knew:

(a)   the words ART, GOOD and REAL are bigger than a lot of folk would have us believe;

(b)   I didn't have to believe everything I was told; and

(c)   anything starting with *women canny* stunk like a month-old kipper.

My mother was dead.
I had not seen my sister for years.

I started writing.

Janice Galloway (born 1956) is a writer. She was born and raised in Ayrshire and now lives in Glasgow. A version of *Objective Truth and the Grinding Machine or Don't Let the Bastards etc. etc.* was first written in 1994 for the Edinburgh Book Festival.

Lorraine Kelly

&

Childhood Memories

I had a very happy childhood. I spent the first couple of years of my life in a single end in Ballater Street in the Gorbals. When we moved to Bridgeton we really went up in the world with a room and a kitchen and an inside toilet.

I always remember long hot summer days playing football on the street, or kick the can and two man hunt. There was an old railway yard across the road from our tenement which we were all forbidden to enter — which meant, of course, that we spent most of our time there. It was a real adventure playground: piles of wood, disused railtrack, a dark tunnel which we dared each other to run through, screaming and shrieking about hidden monsters. We once found an old rusty knife and convinced ourselves that the rust was really blood and that the knife had been used to commit a terrible murder. I remember how solemn we were, wrapping it up in an old hanky and then hiding it deep in one of the woodpiles.

We also played long, complicated games of Batman and Superman. All of us wore duffel coats — usually bought miles too big so that we would 'grow into them'. Duffel coats are perfect for playing at superheroes. You fasten the flap across your neck, leave your arms out of the sleeves, and you have an instant cape which swells satisfyingly in your wake as you run up and down the street.

The street was our playground — and the 'back' of the tenements. We played at shops with broken clear and green glass as money and tin cans rescued from the rubbish bins and filled with dirt or clabber (a mixture of dirt and water). We used old newspapers to wrap up the messages, and whoever's turn it was to be the shopkeeper would clang an imaginary bell and yell at the top of their voice, 'Come and buy, come and buy now the shop is open.'

We would also dare each other to jump the 'dykes' — broken walls in the back courts that separated the bins. Once I misjudged a leap and crashed to the ground and was knocked unconscious. I remember waking up on the couch in my Grannie's house and being given a glass of Irn Bru with a great dod of ice cream floating on the top for being so brave.

Lorraine Kelly is a television presenter and personality.

Maureen Beattie

Stage-Struck

People often ask me if, when I was growing up, there was a moment when I suddenly realised I wanted to be an actress.

I suppose you could argue that, as among the many careers which took my fancy as a child were veterinary surgery, the Catholic sisterhood and, of course, ballet dancing, the moment came when I discovered just how many Higher Grades you needed to begin studying as a vet, or when my Mum explained to me that it really wasn't possible to be a part-time-nun-part-time-ballet-dancer as they were both professions you had to dedicate your whole life to. (I did have a bit of a problem with this one, as I had just seen *The Singing Nun* with Debbie Reynolds and reckoned that if she could sing and be a nun...)

In truth, I believe my fate was sealed at Perth Theatre one afternoon when I was about five years old. My Dad, as the up-and-coming young comedian, Johnny Beattie, was starring in the variety summer season at Perth Rep. This particular afternoon I had been, as usual, watching rehearsals — lapping up the glamour of it all and longing to be part of it. The number being rehearsed involved the entire company, so when tea-break was called and everyone flopped down on the stage and in the stalls for a well-earned rest, I saw my chance to shine.

I toddled up onto the stage, found a suitable space among the recumbent bodies of the company, struck what I imagined was a dramatic and attention-grabbing pose, and then threw myself into a spirited Highland Fling, accompanying myself by singing 'Marie's Wedding'. At the end of this impromptu cabaret no doubt my audience were almost speechless with hilarity, but all I heard was the very gratifying sound of cheering and applause.

Danny Regan, who was the producer of the show, called up from the stalls to ask me why I had put out my arms and sung louder at the end of my song-and-dance. I fixed him with a pitying look and replied, 'You always do that so that people know you've finished and they can clap!' My Dad reckons that was the point of no return.

Maureen Beattie has worked in theatres all over Scotland, in London's West End and with the Royal Shakespeare Company, as well as creating major television roles in *Casualty* and *Bramwell*.

Sally Magnusson

Pride of Place

Rutherglen is a royal burgh. I know this because my mother rarely stopped telling us. Glasgow was the big greedy neighbour with a predilection, which Rutherglen was always resisting, for annexing brave little burghs. Rutherglen was ancient, Rutherglen was special, Rutherglen was favoured by kings, Rutherglen had a charter going back to 1126. I think I drank in Rutherglen's glory with my mother's milk.

By the time regionalisation allowed the city to swallow up this stout burgh at last in one great ruthless gulp, our family had already moved to the country. But my mother's indignation simmered quietly from a distance. Her pride remained fierce. Rutherglen was where her Highland-born grandmother had come as a widow to escape the fetid air of the Gorbals; she used to stride along the Main Street in her long, black widow's weeds, with a black hat perched on her piled hair and a rolled-up umbrella in her hand, her head held so high they called her the Duchess. Rutherglen was where my mother's father courted her mother in Alexander's Chairwork, where he worked as a wood machinist and she as a French polisher. It was where my mother and her twin sister were born in a single-room tenement in East Main Street, the midwife only charging an extra ten shillings over the two-guinea fee for dealing with the unexpected arrival of my mother, too wizened a scrap of humanity to be worth more than ten bob. It was where she went to school, where she huddled in the air-raid shelter as German bombers whined over the Clyde, where she wrote the essay in the English class at Rutherglen Academy that led to her first job on the *Sunday Post*.

These roots made her partisan with a passion. Everything about Rutherglen was better and older than anywhere else. It was a source of deep satisfaction to her that it used to have jurisdiction over much of Glasgow, that its importance as a medieval port was greater, that its pavements were wider. Yes, she was even proud of its pavements. 'This one takes twelve prams across,' my mother liked to boast, as we tagged along the Main Street behind her. Trust her to have measured it, so she could tell us that not only did William Wallace once attend a meeting of the Scottish Parliament in Rutherglen, but where else could that many prams stand abreast on one pavement?

I never cared a toss for her pavements. I was lumpishly incurious about why she felt for this place so fiercely. Rutherglen for me was merely a happy playground. But when I look back now on the endless summers of my childhood, it is her anecdotes and her enthusiasms that give them their grain and texture, her pride that begins to kindle my own. The freckled tomboy racing thoughtlessly around our patch of Calderwood Road with sisters, brothers and pals was part of some greater continuum of town and family, and I can barely see the one without the other.

Maybe this is my imagination making compensation for the sheer banality of my memories. Did I really do nothing but play outside in sunny streets from morning to night, with an occasional foray inside to act out scenes from the television cowboy series *The Virginian*, which involved arranging the long living-room curtains round some chairs, pulling guns on one another and then shouting, 'Trampas, you're hurt. Someone get help quickly!'?

Were Saturdays really as mundanely idyllic as I see them now, a gang of children tearing across the road to Brownlee's sweetie shop to spend our pocket money and then sit chewing sticky white mojoes on the low wall of the power station next door?

I do remember that power station, though. It was a squat, concrete structure with a little plantation of bushes around it whose pungent, heady scent I will never forget. In later years I have sometimes been assaulted by that same fragrance drifting on the evening air from a stranger's garden, and have stood entranced, engulfed in the memories of summer evenings playing among their furry green leaves and red blossoms in the minuscule grounds of the power station. Hide-and-seek was a favourite, and so was a variation on chases which obliged you to choose a punch or a kiss from your captor. Since the local talent was a mite limited at that age, this was a game which invariably promised more than it delivered. The evenings were regularly rent by ringing declarations in Joan of Arc tones that 'any punch would be better than a kiss from YOU'. In one of the more perverse triumphs of hope over experience, we played this day after day.

Across the road was the cow-field, where you went to climb trees, swing from branches and plan military campaigns. I suspect it was a rather scraggy affair as fields went, full of bogs and cow-pats and always in the shade of the trees, but we loved our cowie. We played there long into the dusk and no-one ever worried. I think it's a housing estate now.

The junction where five streets met was our football pitch. Can there really have been so few cars 30 years ago that our games could straddle a big junction and be so little disturbed? It was the bus we had to look out for, the big red double-decker that used to swing down the hill and round the corner to the stop outside our garden.

There were two conductresses who worked this route, one blonde and one dark, both ravishingly beautiful, I thought. If the bus were quiet, they would invite us in for a hurl to the other side of Rutherglen. The great thrill was to be allowed to stand on a seat and press the bell, or turn the handle on the heavy black ticket machine. The bus would amble through the town and end up at Bankhead, where my grandfather had once been janitor at the primary school and dreamed of the education he had missed himself. While the driver snoozed and the conductress unwrapped her sandwiches, there was time to wander along the burn that led past the back of my Grandma's council house in Milrig Road, before the bus turned round and we headed for home.

Back along the Main Street the bus crawled, past the town hall where a telegram declaring 'Independence Maintained' had them dancing in the streets in 1912 after the House of Lords turned down another of Glasgow's attempts to annex the town; past the spot where my grandfather once got twopence from a cattle trader for holding his horse; past the place where my mother got lost at the age of three in a busy grocer's shop called Perks and walked all by herself to her Auntie Betty's house which she recognised by the curtains, something that greatly affronted Auntie Betty because it looked as if she had the same curtains up all the time, which of course she had; past the shop where my father suddenly stopped the Hillman Imp one day and said, 'Let's go and buy something nice' and bought us a packet of long, fat chocolate biscuits oozing the most delicious green, minty filling I had ever tasted.

Rutherglen — a royal burgh with nearly 900 years of memories. And a few of them are mine.

Sally Magnusson (born 1955) is a journalist, television and radio broadcaster and writer.

Anne Mackenzie

Lord of the Flies

When I think about my years at primary school on Lewis, for some reason it's the outcasts I remember.

One boy — let's call him Murdo — springs to mind immediately. He was undersized, poorly dressed and heroically scruffy, and his skin was somehow just a bit too tanned so that no one could really be sure whether he was weather-beaten or just grimy. Of course, like all children, we chose the dirt theory.

But it wasn't just his appearance that held Murdo apart — his family put the lid on his fate. They were a large, rambunctious, carefree brood: the parents, two girls and countless, slightly larger versions of Murdo. His eldest brother was called Murdo, too, in fact, but the reasoning — that they were each named after different Murdos — was island logic and seemed quite normal to all of us. It was rather their attitude to life that set them apart: work just didn't come into their philosophy at all, while, it was widely suspected, unspecified nefarious activities did. In a small community like ours that suspicion gave them their set role to play: the village bad boys. It was, in many ways, a peculiarly tolerant society. The family were never ostracised by the adults, but their difference and the vague contempt in which they were held were easily discernible to children.

Murdo really had only one chance of acceptance, and that was intelligence because, for some reason, academic skill seemed to give credibility points in the playground in a Lewis school. But Murdo didn't seem to be gifted there either, so the fact that he never seemed to mind that no other boys would play with him, that no one spoke to him at the Intervals, the fact that he never even seemed to notice, was put down to pure stupidity. Now I wonder at his resilience.

Yet the boys were never particularly cruel about it; they simply ignored Murdo in a matter-of-fact kind of way; the girls on the other hand turned ostracism into an art form.

You have to understand that the school was very small: the largest class had seven children in it and each schoolroom held three classes. As a result, intense small communities of females formed, although strangely, the boys seemed less inclined to herd together. In each classroom though, one girl tended to lead and ours was Shona, a girl in the class above me: bright, pretty and imbued with that blithe confidence born into some children. Everyone wanted to be her friend, and not to be her friend was the Mark of Cain. Generally, the outcasts were very predictable and they each took their turn, one at a time. The girl with a stammer, devoted for some odd reason to Lulu, the girl who was just too small for her age, the girl who was too fat, and I took my turn, too, since I wore glasses to correct a lazy eye.

It was a miserable experience for children desperate, as we all were, to belong. There was no physical bullying, but all of the eight other girls I remember would gather together giggling in the playground, comparing pop magazines (*Fab 208* was the one to have), enjoying themselves ostentatiously and, of course, sneering and talking very loudly about the outcast. I saw it from both sides which made my eventual rehabilitation into Shona's favour, belonging to the group again, a time of huge rejoicing. After that, the fact that I was reasonably bright seemed to negate the unfortunate presence of my glasses; indeed, Shona appeared to like me.

But then a girl arrived to upset this established order: an outsider in every sense. All of us had joined the school at four or five, had lived in the village all our lives, but Katie Ann came from The Mainland and she was more different than any of us.

Shona was predictable: she took one look at Katie Ann and instinctively, I suppose, saw a victim. So the new girl, acceptably pretty and acceptably bright as she was, spent every playtime in the first weeks of her time at the school sitting on a step alone, while the rest of us — the nine other girls in her room — paraded our togetherness and her apartness.

I don't really know why I did it because I was far from courageous. Perhaps my own ostracism had dimmed in my memory, perhaps it was the dawning of the disastrously over-developed sense of empathy that's plagued me through my life, but one day, a Thursday I remember, I went over and sat down and talked to Katie Ann. Her astonishment was probably as great as Shona's. This had never happened to the one singled out before. But she gabbled eagerly to me in an accent I could barely understand and I remember how warmed I felt by her gratitude. In any case, by the time the bell rang ten minutes later to summon us back into the classroom, I shared her exile.

I don't know if I expected the others to follow my example or not, certainly they didn't. But for the first time, two girls were ostracised together and by necessity we became each other's Best Friend. For two months that summer in fact, we spent all the Intervals together and played together after school, hanging around the village, walking, talking. Looking back, we didn't actually have a lot in common and Katie Ann was older than me by almost three years, but we clung to each other: she and I against the world.

Then one Monday I walked into the classroom to see Katie Ann at her desk surrounded by laughing, animated girls with Shona at the centre of them, and when the bell rang for the morning Interval, Katie Ann ignored me like everyone else. I sat alone, and for the first time I suppose I experienced the true misery of betrayal.

My solo exile didn't last particularly long — only a week or two — then the girl with the stammer took my place as Shona got bored. Shona and Katie Ann became inseparable, but still, no one ever spoke to Murdo. (All names have been changed.)

Anne Mackenzie is a news broadcaster and television journalist.

Neelam Bakshi

1974

On New Year's Day 1974, I was on a flight to India, via Paris and Teheran. I was 13, and was travelling with my sister, Neena, who was 9. Although our parents were Indian, I was born in Kenya and came to Scotland when I was two. It was our first visit to India, the place other Scottish people thought was 'back home' for me.

My parents had made a sudden decision to send us to India where we could go to my cousin, Kanwal's, wedding. I had got my passport after some fancy footwork. We sent for a naturalisation certificate making me British. (I had previously been a 'British Protected Person of Kenya' but hadn't noticed any particular protection when we arrived in Britain as immigrants.) Instead of my Kenyan birth certificate that had been lost in one of our many house moves, a letter from my school confirmed my existence. (Nowadays I keep my passport up to date in case I am asked for my birth certificate.)

India welcomed us with dust and the smell of dry city. Our uncle had come to take us to Old Delhi where we could meet one set of relatives. It was dawn, and the city was alive and colourful with street sellers for every possible need setting up for the day. Old Delhi never seemed to have experienced a street sweeper, cows wandered freely through the streets, and the pungent, acrid smell of the city struck me as I wondered if I would be able to breathe. The family lived in one room and a back-yard, with outside toilet — a ceramic hole in the ground, Indian-style, enclosed by wooden walls and a door with a rusted bolt. My mind played with the unanswerable question of how the family had reached the size of five children, all now adults. It was my first encounter with Tony, only a few years older than myself, charming, beaming, loving — my cousin with Down's Syndrome and few words. He loved to ride trains, and once was lost for several months, reaching East India and being adopted by a family there. They were sorely disappointed when my aunt and uncle tracked him down.

The first weekend, we visited Agra and met more relatives, including cousins only a few years older than ourselves, with friends in the army and access to a jeep. We travelled in the jeep, visiting one cinema, and then popping into another owned by a friend where we caught the climax of the popular young romantic hit, *Bobby* (quite appropriate for at least one friendship that would never be able to mature).

We visited the site of the Moghul city of Fatehpur Sikri, and saw the Taj Mahal by moonlight, an experience never to be forgotten. However many photographs you see, nothing prepares you for its breathtaking beauty. As the marble white structure looms over you, set against a velvet ultramarine sky where the stars echo the marble, a haunting image is created. The symmetrical beauty of the building with its four minarets and water gardens draws you into its spell. The marble was cold on my bare feet. I tied a piece of red string inside, through the fretwork, as a wish that I would return.

The holiday took us to New Delhi where we stayed among a more affluent family, in a three-storey detached house. We knew they were affluent — they had a western-style toilet and a refrigerator.

Then we travelled to Jodhpur where my uncle, an officer in the Air Force, was stationed and where we got a taste of military life. The men were young, handsome, polite — and wild. Living in a war zone near the borders of China and Pakistan, these young men lived lives of fun, knowing their next mission might be their last.

My insight was closer than most. One cousin, Kanwal, was marrying Deepak, an officer; the other, Seema, had recently met his friend Monty, the officer whom she would later marry. Neena had

had an accident on a cousin's bike in Agra so her early experience in Jodhpur was coloured with visits to the military hospital for penicillin injections. The house had grilles for windows, and we had a daily visit from a small animal known affectionately as Baby Lizard who clung to the grille during daylight hours like a silent chaperone.

During our time in Jodhpur we visited the fort and the Palace, where we watched peacocks roaming the grounds. I gasped at the opulence of the indoor swimming pool. It was hard to believe all this was still privately owned and the Rajah was in residence. Jodhpur was more rural, bustling and honest, with camels a regular sight in this town in the Rajasthani desert. We went to the market where I watched my aunt haggling like a pro, dropping the price to half the original. It was years before I understood that paying the first price asked was the signal identifying you as a tourist.

Stalls sold freshly cooked snacks — sweet and savoury, from freshly juiced sugar cane to gol guppas, fried hollow crisp pastry balls with spicy dipping liquid. We saw one stall where a man sold containers made by pounding and hammering together old tin cans — an entirely new interpretation of thrift and recycling. On another occasion my father, who had arrived in India two weeks behind us, asked a trader for some lentils. To his astonishment, the trader directed him to another stall saying those lentils were cleaner (with fewer pieces of grit) than at his stall. An early lesson in business ethics for me.

My father decided to have some fun at my expense. He asked a villager if they could tell what I was. His reply will never leave me: 'She looks like one of us, but speaks and dresses like a memsahib.' I already knew that in Scotland I was seen as an unwanted outsider whose home was in India. What a way to learn that I didn't belong to India either. The different kind of homelessness that my generation has struggled with has, perhaps, allowed us to become true multiculturalists and citizens of the world because we have no parochial attachments to individual nations.

A chance remark revealed to my uncle that, unusually for a Western teenager, I had a strong belief in my Hindu faith. Consequently, a special trip was arranged taking in the holy sites of Hardwar and Rishikesh, in the Himalayas, complete with the chance to bathe in the Ganges and fulfil the dream and duty of every Hindu. Women bathed, clothed, in a cave away from the sight of men. We were near the source of the Ganges and were not concerned about what might be thrown in down-river. We visited temple after temple, each with a resident priest. We seemed to stop every couple of miles to get out of the tonga, the horse-drawn vehicle we were using. I saw how villagers worshipped, learning something about the simplicity and honesty of their faith. In Glasgow, by contrast, they struggled to set up a temple that met everyone's needs except local residents whose objections were finally met in court by little old Indian ladies who demanded the right to a place to worship — but we had no priest on site for 15 years.

The visit into the foothills of the Himalayas had led us to more family, living in Dehra Dun. I was surprised to find close family I had never heard of before, again with teenage children to whom Neena and I could relate. One cousin played veena, a stringed musical instrument, and accordion, which helps me understand where my daughter's musical gifts come from.

Everywhere we went, there were beggars and street people. In Delhi, as dusk settled, street braziers began to glow and tents went up. The street dwellers had little in the way of material goods, and plenty of dignity and self-pride as they washed on the streets, and cooked their meagre rations in gleaming brass pots. Children in rags begged at railway stations and I was never able to put their faces, with large, haunting, soft brown eyes, out of my mind. Nor have I been able to reconcile the harshness which indigenous Indians displayed as they ignored the beggars or shooed them away — a practice born of pragmatism, I'm sure.

This contrasted outrageously with the splendour of Kanwal's wedding in Delhi. Items for the dowry included a refrigerator and sewing machine, and the fruit seemed to have been grown in a giant's orchard. The pomegranates were red as rosy apples, the apples were as big as melons, and the clothes came in all the shades of the rainbow sprinkled with the glitter of sequins and threads embroidered traditionally by hand. Seema (nicknamed Babli) and I had our hair done professionally in styles that added ten years to our ages and nothing to our temperament.

We helped Kanwal stand, supporting her when she threatened to topple over because the weight of gold thread on her sari was so overwhelming. The groom was dressed in Western suit and trousers but wore the traditional head-dress that veiled his face from his bride as hers was from him. Following tradition, Deepak had ridden in on a white horse. We also followed tradition. We hid the groom's shoes and demanded payment for their return, which was in addition to the paper-thin gold rings we had already received as sister and cousin-sister to the bride. We went further than tradition when we sat, giggles and innocence alternating, as we sewed the groom's jacket to his cushion whilst he sat listening to the solemn intonations of the priest conducting the ceremonies. He foiled our work by standing up abruptly, uncertain of what we were doing but knowing something was up. And he had got his brother to bring a spare pair of shoes — not playing fair at all.

A few days after the wedding we returned to Jodhpur, travelling by train in different compartments. Babli and I shared the top of a three-tier bunk (just as well we were bosom-mates by then as well as related) and there were just as many without bunks as in them, squatting on the floor getting breaths of air from the open doors as we travelled from Jodhpur to Delhi where our visit would end. The conversation was brilliant, and we got to taste the famous warm milk from Mathura, bought at the station in disposable clay cups — you toss them out of the window. But there really is nothing like third-class rail travel in India, and if there is, I hope I never find it.

We returned to Britain having spent six weeks away. It seemed a lifetime. Everything was the same and yet not quite the same. Britain was grey, and dark and wet. I got back to school, unhappy at the thought of the backlog to catch up. I had acquired international pen-pals, two very deep friendships, and a myriad memories.

Significantly, I had found a part of myself — rooted in India and yet not of India. I knew more about my Indian-ness and my family's history in the flesh and I also knew that I did not belong there. I was a Scottish Asian, who spoke a little of my parents' language, but didn't read and write it. My Hindu faith was no more than that — faith alone — with little access to the philosophy or a spiritual guide, although my community had begun to provide opportunities to share in the rituals. The visit had made me thirst for knowledge and ways of seeing how to integrate myself as a Scottish Asian. I eventually took religious studies at university as a way of filling some of the gaps, and understood that an arranged marriage was not for me — especially not with someone from the Indian sub-continent who might not be willing to allow the developing independent streak to mature.

I have not been back to India yet. Now my daughter, Ambika, is 14. When she travels, will she also find a part of herself in India or is it different for children of mixed heritage? Is it a very individual experience? I don't know, but I want her to see the Taj, and feel the spirit of India as I did. I want her to meet my cousins' children who are now as old as she, and I want her to use her visit to sustain her in that journey called life as I did, another Scottish Asian child spending her life in Scotland.

Neelam Bakshi (born 1960) is Policy Adviser (Equalities) on Fife Council and an occasional broadcaster. She was the first black woman councillor in Scotland (Strathclyde Regional Council 1990-1996).

Blythe Duff

What's in a Name?

Most people can recall their first day at school. I remember two teachers standing in the assembly hall holding a plate of jellybeans — very good psychology. The headmistress announced that she was going to shout out each child's name. They were to go to the teacher bearing jellybeans whereupon they would be taken to the class for a picnic. My eyes lit up at the thought of ice cream and jelly, sandwiches, crisps, orange juice. Fantastic! School was going to be a triumph after all. I sat clutching my mother's hand as the girls' names were called out.

'Angela Anderson?' (red hair, quite plump, runny nose).

'Lesley Boyle?' (swinging ponytail, yellow wellies).

'Lyn Favour?' (very tall for her age, very blonde for her age).

I recall that in Primary Three, Lyn swallowed a sixpence. The teacher had to turn her upside down and slap her on the back, whereupon the sixpence fell to the floor. High drama, I remember at the time.

I was just thinking it was a good job that the girls were first on the list — if Gary Meldrum had got those jellybeans there was no hope for the rest of us. The roll-call continued, 'And finally, Susan Watson? Now for the boys.' My mother's face dropped, she shot out of her chair with her hand up. 'Please Miss' (I think the whole school thing had got to her), 'I have another little girl here.'

'Oh? What's her name?'

'Blythe... Blythe Duff. Blythe Watson Drummond Duff.' It was all or nothing.

'Oh, yes. D'you know we were uncertain whether Blythe was a girl's name or a boy's name so we just put her at the end.'

My mother sat down with a sigh of relief as I ran up to Miss Laing who, thankfully, was refilling the jellybean plate.

We waved goodbye to our mothers and marched in a line to our class. We found our desks, played in the sandpit, rearranged building blocks and looked at the animal alphabet around the wall. I was thinking that some time soon the jelly was sure to arrive. Suddenly, Miss Laing placed an orange triangle filled with milk on the desk and before we knew it, it was duffel coats on and out the door. 'Some picnic!', I exclaimed to my mother as she pulled my new white socks up around my needle-thin legs. Primary school never did live up to my expectations.

My name continued to cause confusion. My father worked at the Rolls Royce factory in East Kilbride. Every year they had a rather posh Christmas party with cartoons, games — the lot. Santa would come, as usual, bearing gifts. I remember one year my sister, Sylvia, did very well. A Sindy doll. With a complete change of clothes. I mean anything was possible! I ripped my present open trying to guess what it might be. It was too small for Tiny Tears. It was just too big for a Spirograph. It was a Tonka truck filled with chocolate Santas. OK, so the chocolate Santas crossed all gender but, unless I could convince my sister that Sindy was destined for a career in the TA, there was no hope of peace and joy at Christmas. I stuffed the chocolate Santas down my throat.

I managed to trade the truck for Kerplunk. Not a bad deal, actually.

Blythe Duff (born 1962) is an actress who enjoys working in theatre and television. She is best known as D.S. Jackie Reid in STV's detective series *Taggart*.

Gavin Hastings

❦

Happy Days

My formative school years were invaluable, not only in igniting my interest in all games, but in keeping me out of mischief. I am the product of many dedicated people, who saw to it that my interest in sport, and in rugby football in particular, was aroused.

I suppose it all began at George Watson's College when, from the age of five, I used to play football in the primary school playground. I remember the school janitor lining us up prior to going into our classrooms in the morning, to give prizes for the cleanest pair of shoes. My Dad used to be very finicky about these things and he would always polish our shoes every morning, so I was lucky. I used to take an old pair of training shoes to change into as soon as I arrived, to play football in, and when we lined up for inspection I quickly got my clean shoes out of my bag, and used to win lots of Mars bars, which aroused some envy in my schoolmates. It was really thanks to my Dad, who taught me at an early age the value of being well turned out.

These were formative times and we played a lot of football in the playgrounds. Later, when my Dad became a committee member of the Watsonian Football Club, he used to run the line with the seconds, thirds and fourths on a Saturday afternoon. All his pals had kids roughly the same age and we used to go down to play football at Myreside. Nowadays, I see the children of my contemporaries, Euan Kennedy and Roger Baird, all doing the same things that we once did. Often it was freezing outside and pitch dark, yet there we were, playing with a rugby ball or a football, while our Dads were drinking up in the club house. Then it was a case of going off to the chippy and getting a fish supper on the way home, where we arrived absolutely filthy but happy.

As we got older, we used to play on the adjacent pitch at Myreside during Watsonian home matches but as soon as the goal kicks were being taken on the main pitch I would stop playing and go and watch the goal kickers, who fascinated me. We used to play a game called gaining ground, with two or more players in each team. It was simply a question of kicking the ball up field and making as much yardage as possible; if you caught the ball in field you were allowed to advance ten yards and punt it, and, as soon as you were within goal kicking range, you could place the ball and attempt to kick it between the posts for a score. I probably had more success then than I had in 1994 in the Five Nations Championship!

We started playing rugby in Primary Six, when we were 10-years-old, but for me it all began disastrously, for one day I was playing football in the school playground when a teacher drove past where he should not have been. I collided with his car, ripped my leg and needed about 15 stitches inserted in the wound. I was devastated, for I missed my first couple of months of rugby. But there is always a silver lining — the teacher whose car I collided with was the rugby master in charge of our year. Within about a week of starting he had made me captain of the side, which was very amusing and showed that he had a conscience. Luck, it seemed, was always on my side, and that year we played seven games and won all seven matches.

During the next few years we played all the other rugby-playing schools in Scotland, as well as our Edinburgh rivals, Stewart's Melville and Heriot's, and we always seemed to have close matches. Strangely, not many of us progressed from that era and only David Sole and myself advanced from our contemporaries all the way through from the Scottish schoolboys team to the full national side. It is amazing when you see players who had so much talent at school suddenly lose their ambition when they leave and discover beer, women and work. I guess they have found different priorities in their lives, but I thought that many of them wasted their natural resources. I can never understand why people do not make the most of their innate talent and work hard to fully develop their potential. After all, life is not a dress rehearsal, it is for real.

I began to understand and commit myself to rugby pretty seriously when I got into the First XV in my fifth year, which was probably the norm; the better fifth year players always made it into the First XV. Getting into the Firsts when I was 16 was a great thrill. I was playing stand off in those days, for all my early rugby was played in that position, but then I got injured in a midweek game and went to Donald Scott (Mr Scott or Sir, in those days) who was in charge of the school First XV, and told him that I did not think I could play at stand off. We were short with a couple of injuries, so he said, 'I'll play you at full back,' and I have been there ever since.

I have a lot to thank Donald Scott for, that is for sure.

Donald Scott had ten caps for Scotland in the early fifties, and played in the infamous 44-0 disaster against the Springboks in 1951. I am afraid that was superseded by our recent 51-15 beating by the All Blacks. We never reminded Donald about the Springboks match when we were at school, for he was a ruthless teacher. I remember that once he got out a belt, two inches wide and about half an inch thick, and said, 'If there is any messing around, this is what is going to happen', then proceeded to take a chunk out of a very thick mahogany door. Bloody hell! There was no messing about after that. Donald was a strict teacher, but he was a good man. He used to run one of the school boarding houses and all the boys from Donald's bug hut, as we used to call his house, were fairly well behaved.

From *High Balls and Happy Hours* (written with Clem Thomas)

Gavin Hastings (born 1962) played rugby for Watsonians and captained the Scottish National Rugby side during the Five Nations Championship of 1994.

Eric Black

❦

Football Dreams

As a boy living in the Lanarkshire town of East Kilbride, my friends and I would pass every waking hour playing football in the streets and parks near our homes. We would analyse and re-analyse every game whether Premier League or, more importantly, the Scottish National Team's exploits. We dreamed of the day that we, too, would be professional footballers playing at the highest level and scoring goals in front of 80,000 roaring supporters on the hallowed turf of Hampden Park just like our heroes — Kenny Dalgleish, Dennis Law and Joe Jordan.

Many an evening was spent arguing and discussing the merits and flaws of the footballing stars of the day. Each of us had a particular favourite and we donated much of our time to emulating their achievements on the field. To us, wee boys, these people were god-like untouchables!

How lucky we were without realising it, to be able to play in the streets of our town without fear of cars disturbing our game. At weekends and holidays we would carry our games on until late in the evening and even into darkness without our mothers' having to worry for our safety. Unfortunately, this is not the case in today's modern society.

As we grew older we began to play in various teams like the school team and local boys' team. Here we had the perfect vehicle to show off and impress our peers with the movements we had practised so diligently during our long hours together. Failure was commonplace, but our enthusiasm and appetite for football never diminished. The dream of glory was always firmly fixed in our minds.

As we grew up, all the members of our street team went their separate ways. I went on to pursue a career as a professional football player, realising my boyhood dreams. But I particularly remember one young lad, who lived round the corner from me, showing great promise as a youngster. He also went on to play the game at a professional level. In fact, I still bump into him occasionally. I sometimes see him playing, and he re-enacts those very same skills we practised all those years ago in the street. Maybe you've heard of him? Ally McCoist.

Eric Black (born 1963) played professional football for Aberdeen F.C. and Metz F.C. (France) before retiring due to a back injury. He now works with Celtic F.C. as Football Development Director.

Evelyn Glennie

❀

A Very Ordinary Childhood

People are often astonished when I tell them that I had a very ordinary childhood. My life was like that of any other local child brought up on a farm, with lots of fresh air and outdoor activities, and the usual routine of school and homework, while fitting in as much fun as possible with my brothers and friends.

The farm was the centre of our lives and each year followed the same pattern of care for crops and animals. We never took holidays away from Hillhead and even on Christmas Day Mum and Dad had to break off whatever they were involved in to feed the beasts and attend to our poultry. When I was very little my only contribution to farm work was careering up and down the henhouse on my tiny blue and red tricycle, terrifying the hens, to my father's secret and rather wicked amusement. Later I took a more responsible attitude, collecting and sorting the eggs, and helping to feed the young calves. My favourite job was looking after the 'caddy' lambs which had been abandoned by their mothers. At one time we had a large flock of sheep, which meant that Dad and the boys were often up all through the wretchedly cold winter nights during the lambing season. The caddies were handed over to me for bottle feeding, and if I managed to rear them successfully I would get the money when they were sold. This was sometimes as much as £45, so was well worth the effort. They usually lived in the stable in a little pen stacked with straw, but if they were very weak we would keep them warm in the kitchen on an old rug. I used to get very attached to my wee charges, who obviously regarded me as 'mum' and, even when they were too old for bottle feeding, would follow me around the fields, bleating pathetically and making me feel terribly mean.

I loved all the farm creatures except the three geese. They lived in the courtyard and relished a good chase; as soon as they caught me they would push me over and nip my bottom hard, a terrifying experience for a toddler. Perhaps because I was surrounded by living playmates of all shapes and sizes, I had little interest in toys.

I did have a small pink teddy bear who spent most of his time hanging by his ears from the washing line, as I was always pestering Mum to drop him in the suds on washing day. I also had a huge doll which I've still got somewhere, although she long ago lost all her hair; but I preferred teddy bears to dolls, and cats were best of all, they were so warm and soft to cuddle. Aunt Evelyn gave me 'the doll' as I somewhat unimaginatively called it; she and Uncle Jim had no children of their own and used to spoil us with presents and treats. It was always fun to visit them, as she worked in a large house at Downside which had huge grounds and woodlands where we could run around and collect pine cones.

We took time off as a family whenever we could. We never went to the cinema or theatre; in fact my first visit to the cinema was when I went to Bristol for a percussion concert at the age of 16. Our trips were very much confined to the community and districts near the farm. A favourite treat was to go for a 'run' — an evening drive in summer exploring new roads and countryside, and stopping off for a 'chew', an ice-cream, in one of the little villages around Turriff. I always had to sit in the middle between the two boys and remember the bother of where to put my legs as they grew too long to dangle over the hump of the brake box. Less popular was the weekly visit to church, where Mum would install herself at the organ and the rest of us would sit on a hard wooden pew which we shared with an elderly couple. I was always positioned behind a pillar and could see very little of the proceedings; the pew was also extremely uncomfortable and I used to long for our neighbours to stay at home to give me an excuse to borrow their cushion and doze off in comfort.

My Sunday best was a burgundy velvet dress handed down by one of my many cousins. Nearly all my clothes were hand-me-downs when I was a little girl. I also had a grey coat with fur trims round the cuffs and collar, and a lovely warm hand muff where I used to keep a secret store of sweets to munch through the service. These 'dressed-up' clothes were only for special occasions. I usually wore trousers and dungarees, and was the despair of my mother because I would rarely consent to put on a skirt or dress. I felt happiest in clothes that allowed me to stretch and run and ride my bicycle. Even in winter, outdoor games were favourite with Roger and myself, playing snowballs and speeding down the hills on our flat wooden sledges, warmly wrapped in woolly scarves and jumpers and our colourful 'toorie' hats with a bobble on top.

Winter inevitably brought havoc, with loss of power, and no means of communication except by foot as all the roads were blocked. My father would clear a way with his snow plough, and shopping trips to the nearby village of Methlick would often be done by tractor. Dad would drive and Mum, the boys and I would bump along behind in the cart. I always had a store of snowballs, and would lie low and then pop up to hurl them at unsuspecting passers-by. It always amused me to see Mum in the cart — our church organist trying to look dignified as she bounded along with a pack of unruly children.

The countryside was stunning in winter; the brilliant whiteness of the land glittered morning and night with the sun and the moon, and I often thought that it was a shame that people existed in the midst of this perfection, ploughing through it and making everything look haggard. Each year I used to build a family of snowmen under the kitchen window, ranging from tiny to as big as I could push, with carrot noses, stone eyes and straw hair, and dressed in Dad's old scarves and hats. At night, the light would stream out of the window, gleaming on their pale bodies and casting strange shadows across the snowy lawn. A less popular activity was the construction of a 'slidey', a treacherous patch of ice from the house door to the coal and tool sheds, so that everyone was forced to cross its shimmering surface at some time of the day.

We had to live through many long winter nights with no power. The only heat was from the glow of the fire, and we would play cards and dominoes by candlelight before shivering our way early to bed. By the time I was 12-years-old, I couldn't hold conversations in the dark, and we would shine a torch on each person's face as they spoke so that I could lip-read. Colin still jokes about all the nasty things they were able to say about me, without my being able to hear. Sometimes the power cuts would last for days and Mum would be struggling to cook rather stodgy basic meals on a tiny gas cooker that took hours to heat up the food.

We had lots of visitors and, as a tiny child, I particularly loved it when Dad's friends called in. They would pick me up and whizz me through the air, or let me hobble round the room with my feet on their big boots. I liked to climb on their knees or ride piggyback, and was never afraid to make frank personal observations. 'Skin!' I would shout, discovering the inevitable bald patch at the back of their heads, and they would tickle me in punishment until I begged for mercy. I am grateful to those forthright farming folk for providing me with a ready fund of colourful swearwords which I happily rehearse when having a particularly bad practice session.

From *Good Vibrations: My Autobiography* (with Pamela Norris)

Evelyn Glennie OBE is a world-famous solo percussionist.

Stephen Hendry

❦

The Christmas Present

Irene Hendry was remembering how it all started. 'Stephen got his first snooker table when he was twelve. It was for Christmas, and just two weeks before his 13th birthday. At the time we were staying at my sister's house in Dalgety Bay, Fife. She was in Canada, so we stayed in her house before we bought our own.'

The present was a last-minute decision that was to change all their lives, for Stephen had never played snooker until his parents bought him that table.

'We couldn't think what to get him,' said Irene. 'I was shopping in Dunfermline at the time and saw the table in John Menzies. It cost £137. It was six feet by four feet, and looked smashing, so I went home to Gordon and discussed it with him. He had most other things a boy of his age would want — golf clubs, badminton racket, a football, so we decided to buy him the table.'

'I'll always remember the expression on Stephen's face that Christmas morning. His eyes lit up, and we thought: "We've cracked it. He really likes it." And that was all that mattered to us.'

The 12-year-old liked it, all right. Even now, his eyes widen as he recalls: 'The first time I picked up a snooker cue, I fell in love with the game.'

The table that was to transform his life was put in his bedroom, squashed against a wall, which made some shots difficult. But the boy discovered he had a natural talent.

'I played on that table whenever I could. I would have a hit before I went to school, and I would play on it non-stop when I came home from school, stopping only to have dinner. Within two weeks I had scored a 50 break. I played my dad, and was beating him all the time. I was learning and loving it all, although I don't know if my dad felt the same.

'I wasn't tall then, less than five feet, and had to use the rest frequently. That turned out to be not such a bad thing, because the rest plays such an important part in any player's game. When I started on the professional circuit, I was five feet seven inches. I'm glad I sprang up in the years to follow, because it made playing snooker much easier.

'I realised I might have a future in snooker when I was just 13. Then, at the Classic Snooker Centre in Dunfermline, I hit my first century break. It was a marvellous moment. I was playing with my dad, and after it I went through to tell the club owner. He said: "Were there any witnesses?" Clearly, he didn't believe me, and I don't blame him, for there were not too many 13-year-olds banging in 100 breaks. I knew then that I could play the game.'

Stephen went down to Pontins in Wales, to play in the Under-16s 'Stars of the Future', to find out just how good he really was.

'It proved worthwhile, because I won the tournament. A lot of people were surprised, and I was over the moon. It was also my first money win — £100.

'From then on it was goodbye to school studies. I studied for four O-Levels at Inverkeithing High School, sat two, failed miserably, and got none. It wasn't that I was totally thick, but snooker took up all my spare time. The headmaster, Mr Mackenzie, was very under-standing, and allowed me time off to play in amateur tournaments all over Britain.

'Some of my teachers were a bit disappointed that I was not apply-ing myself as well as I could, and that was understandable. To be honest, some of them thought I was off my head to think a daft wee boy from Scotland was good enough to make the grade in snooker. They must have thought they had a right day-dreamer, a kind of Walter Mitty. But, by that time, I had won a number of tournaments, some worth £500, which wasn't bad for a 15-year-old.'

But for that Christmas present, Stephen might have wound up working in his dad's fruit shop. There's no doubt that the biggest early influence on his career was his parents. 'They let me do just what I wanted — play snooker — and my dad came everywhere with me. He never missed a match.'

From John Docherty, *Remember My Name: The Authorised Biography of Stephen Hendry*

Stephen Hendry (born 1969), ranked World Number One, has won six World and five British Snooker Championships amongst others.

Neil Kempsell

Stephen Loved Having a 'Big Break' Time Away from School

Neil Kempsell (born 1959) is a freelance professional caricaturist, cartoonist and illustrator who enjoys fresh air and malt whisky. He teaches at Edinburgh Art College.

David Coulthard

🌑

Go-karting

Like most people, my childhood memories are filled with nostalgia. Growing up in the beautiful Scottish countryside, life seemed so pure and uncomplicated. Living in a small village where everybody knew each other evoked a great sense of safety and meant that my friends and I had freedom and space to enjoy all the usual childhood activities.

Like most young boys, I began karting with my friends. It seemed a fun thing to do, and it didn't take long to discover that not only did I enjoy the exhilarating feeling of travelling at speed, but I was actually quite good at it. Consequently, I started taking part in go-karting competitions, which resulted in considerable success. It was not long before most of my spare time and practically every weekend was taken up travelling all over the country to compete in various events. Karting was my passion. Often as I lined up on the starting grid I imagined myself in the future poised in a top Formula 1 racing car, waiting to accelerate away into the first corner.

As a result my teenage years turned out to be rather different from those of my school friends. Whilst I might have missed out on some of the typical teenage experiences, my karting made up for it in other ways. In addition to it taking me all over the UK and Europe to compete in events, I got to meet many interesting people, some of whom became good friends. Most of my friends shared my love of karting and were extremely supportive. At the same time they ensured that I kept my feet firmly planted on the ground and maintained my status as simply 'one of the boys'.

My memory is filled with numerous hilarious encounters from my teenage years. As we lived in the remote countryside we were able to hold parties in big old barns, and because they were situated a good distance away from the nearest house, we could play our music as loud as we liked without annoying anyone. Of course, my friends and I always ensured that we invited far more girls than boys and insisted that kissing was always near the top of the agenda. We thought that we were very cool and experienced. In reality — like every teenage boy — we ended up dancing to the girls' tunes!

David Coulthard (born 1971) has won three Formula 1 Grand Prix so far in his career. When not racing, he divides his time between Twynholm and Monaco.

COLLINS

Other Scottish-interest titles available from HarperCollins
Publishers include:

Collins Gems

Famous Scots £3.99
Whisky £3.99
Burns Anthology £3.99
Castles of Scotland £3.99
Clans and Tartans £3.99
Scots Dictionary £3.99

Pocket Reference

Scottish Country Dancing £5.99
Scottish Myths and Customs £5.99
Scottish Surnames £5.99
Cycling in Scotland £3.99
Scotland £3.99
Clans and Tartans £3.99
Whisky £6.99

The Scottish Collection Gift Series

Classic Malts £4.99
Homelands of the Clans £4.99
Scottish Recipes £4.99
Scottish Verse £4.99

Guides

Scotland the Best! The One True Guide £9.99
Edinburgh the Best! £4.99
Glasgow the Best! £4.99
Touring Guide to Scotland £6.99

Other titles

The Collins Scottish Clan and Family Encyclopedia . £30.00
The Scottish Regiments (2nd edition) £9.99
Scots Kith & Kin £4.99